Finding the Right Pieces

A Guide Book for
Personal Relationships

Jack Almeleh, M.D.

Visit our website at www.StillwaterPress.com for more information.

First Stillwater River Publications Edition

ISBN-13: 978-1-946300-73-7
ISBN-10: 1-946300-73-X

Library of Congress Control Number: 2018952142

1 2 3 4 5 6 7 8 9 10

Written by Jack Almeleh, M.D.
Cover design by Kody Lavature

Published by Stillwater River Publications, Pawtucket, RI, USA.

Publisher's Cataloging-In-Publication Data
(Prepared by The Donohue Group, Inc.)

Names: Almeleh, Jack.
Title: Finding the right pieces : a guidebook for personal relationships / Jack Almeleh, M.D.
Description: First Stillwater River Publications edition. | Pawtucket, RI, USA : Stillwater River Publications, [2018]
Identifiers: ISBN 9781946300737 | ISBN 194630073X
Subjects: LCSH: Interpersonal relations--Handbooks, manuals, etc. | Friendship--Handbooks, manuals, etc. | Mate selection--Handbooks, manuals, etc.
Classification: LCC HM1106 .A56 2018 | DDC 302--dc23

This book is intended as general advice and is not a substitute for the advice of a therapist.

DEDICATION

This book is dedicated to my many teachers in life.

First to my parents, especially my mother Rachel Almeleh, who provided me with her view of the world around her, as well as her unconditional love. Secondly, it is dedicated to the Chairman of the Department of Psychiatry where I trained, Dr. R. Bruce Sloane, who allowed me, and all of his psychiatric residents, the freedom to think independently and creatively. And thirdly, to the patients I've treated over the years who taught me how to be a better psychiatrist.

This book is also dedicated to a teacher I never met, my maternal grandmother, Rivka Cohen, who was killed in Auschwitz-Birkenau. Her view of life and her love filtered down through the generations. I wish I had met her.

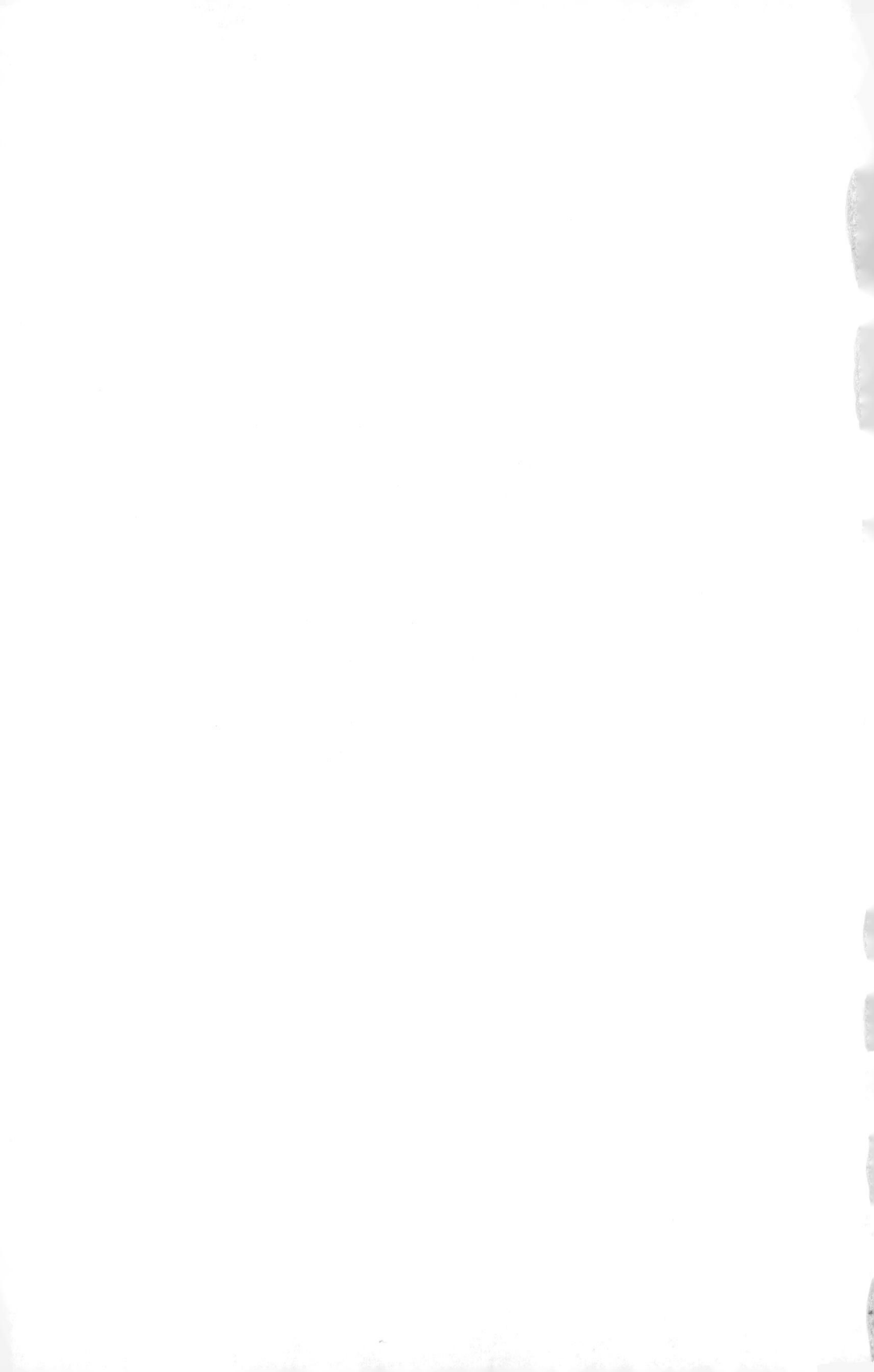

ACKNOWLEDGEMENTS

First I'd like to thank the many patients I treated over the years. My strong desire to help them motivated and forced me to think "outside the box." The therapeutic models presented in this book were not taught to me during my psychiatric residency training but were derived from my experience treating my patients.

Alice and Larry Brauer, very bright friends of mine, read my book and provided support and encouraged me to publish this book, feeling that it would be very helpful to its readers. I also thank Alice for her expert editing.

Jack Karp, another friend of mine, read my book and provided helpful advice.

The illustrations in this book were drawn by Gus Vergara. His talent and patience as we worked together trying to accurately illustrate the concepts presented in this book are very much appreciated. Thank you, Gus.

TABLE OF CONTENTS

INTRODUCTION

The purpose of this book is to present models of relationships—casual relationships, friendships, and romantic relationships—that are easy to understand, and, if kept in mind, can enable the reader to function more comfortably and find fulfilling relationships.

Finding friendships and romantic relationships is not easy. It is often fraught with anxiety, insecurity, and sensitivity to rejection. The goal of this book is to present models of these relationships that can minimize anxiety and sensitivity to rejection, and maximize the chances of finding relationships that are right for you.

Who is right for you as a friend or a romantic partner is right for you, but not necessarily right for someone else. Understanding and applying the concepts presented in this book can enable you to comfortably find the relationships that are best suited for you.

The psychological approach utilized in this book falls into the general category referred to as cognitive psychotherapy. To explain cognitive psychotherapy simply, we can say that we all process things (or "look" at things) in a certain way. The way we look at things can work to our advantage or not. To learn to look at things in a way that is helpful, and that enables us to function better and that can lead to a more fulfilling life, is the goal of cognitive psychotherapy and is the goal of this book.

Ultimately, this book is designed to be therapeutic.

THE JIGSAW PUZZLE PIECE MODEL
OF WHO WE ARE

In this book we use the model of a jigsaw puzzle piece to symbolize who we are. We do this to make easier the understanding of certain concepts that will be presented.

Each of us is unique, and we denote that uniqueness by each of us being represented by a jigsaw puzzle piece—each puzzle piece being different in shape. The shape of our puzzle piece corresponds to our characteristics: our personality, our cultural background, values, interests, sense of humor, level of intelligence, and the type of intelligence we have (intellectual vs. artistic), etc. Some of these characteristics are genetic and some are shaped by our upbringing and our environment. Regardless of the etiology, we all are different and our jigsaw puzzle pieces are different. As unique as we all are, that's how unique our puzzle pieces are.

For various reasons, people may not show the true shape of their jigsaw puzzle piece. They may not be comfortable with who they are, and try not to reveal themselves. Or, indeed, their discomfort with their true self may cause them to present a false picture of themselves. Whatever the reason, sooner or later the true shape of one's jigsaw puzzle piece is shown. As will be explained later in this book, if you are trying to find close friends or a life partner, hiding or misrepresenting your puzzle piece is counterproductive, and a waste of time. Sooner or later the truth comes out and the true shape of a person's jigsaw puzzle piece is revealed.

There are times not showing the true shape of one's jigsaw puzzle piece is common and understandable. For example, when applying for a job or interviewing for college. It's understandable that people will try to appear smarter or perhaps more pleasant than they truly are. In these situations, a person is just trying to "get their foot in the door." They're not trying to establish a long-term personal relationship with the interviewer. But if you're looking to establish a friendship or a romantic relationship, not being who you are is counterproductive. It will lead to disappointment for both parties, and if formed, the relationship will not last.

The shape of someone's jigsaw puzzle piece may change slightly over time if a person changes. But my experience has been that people really don't change that much. But if someone does change, the shape of one's jigsaw puzzle piece changes and new relationships may result. This will be discussed in a later chapter in the book.

BOTTOM LINE: People are different. And in this book, we represent that difference by a unique shape to a person's jigsaw puzzle piece. Showing the true shape of one's jigsaw puzzle piece is an essential first step in finding and establishing long-term satisfying personal relationships. Not showing the shape of one's jigsaw puzzle piece is counterproductive to establishing close friendships and a romantic relationship.

FRIENDSHIPS

We meet many people as we go through life. Some of these individuals will become close friends, and others not. As a psychiatrist, I often wondered what causes an individual to choose a particular person as a close friend and not someone else.

But let's first ask the question, what is a friend?

Put simply, a friend is someone whose company you enjoy. Importantly, you enjoy that person's company because of who that person is—that person's personality, interests, values, etc.—and not for what that person can give you tangibly. In a true friendship, nothing tangible has to be given to you for you to enjoy that person's company. In effect, a friend is someone who winds up giving you nothing more than just being themselves, and as a result, you're happier in their presence.

In biological terms, we can say that a close friendship is a symbiotic relationship. By that we mean, whatever comes out of that person naturally, just by that person living his or her life and being themselves, without actually focusing on giving you anything, adds to your level of pleasure being in that person's company. In effect, a friend can behave in a relatively selfish way, and yet you still enjoy being with that individual.

Our definition of friendship implies that a friendship should require very little, if any, work. This may be contrary to some people's belief that a friend is someone to whom you give a great deal. Giving a lot to a friend may occur in times of a friend's great need, such as illness. But, in the absence of unusual circumstances, little work should be required in a friendship. If a lot of work is required under normal circumstances, the friendship will not last. In effect, a friendship is a symbiotic relationship where two individuals give very little, other than themselves to each other, and both get a great deal back in terms of pleasure. It's two individuals behaving in a relatively selfish way, and yet enjoying each other's company.

But what causes an individual to choose one person as a friend, and not someone else?

In my psychiatric practice I noticed something very interesting. ***When people described their closest friend, they described someone who was very much like themselves.*** They described someone with a similar personality, and similar interests, values, cultural background, level of intelligence, sense of humor, etc. It was uncanny.

Sandra, a patient of mine, was an example of this.

Sandra was a pretty, outgoing young girl who very much enjoyed life. She came to see me because she was having panic attacks.

Sandra worked as a secretary in a very large office. In the course of treatment, and as an aside, she described her best friend at work. Her friend was also a very outgoing young girl who enjoyed life. And, "Oh, by the way," she said, "she has panic attacks, and is Italian just like me."

Of all the diverse people that worked at this very large firm, her closest friend, someone whose company she enjoyed the most, was someone very much like herself. Was it a coincidence? I just couldn't believe it was.

And the clincher was my patient, Paul.

Paul was scheduled to be married in three weeks. He came to see me complaining of severe anxiety and trouble sleeping.

It seemed that Paul had an identical twin brother, Bob. They were best friends, and they did practically everything together their entire lives. As Paul's wedding day approached, his fiancée became increasingly uncomfortable with Paul's close relationship with his twin brother Bob, and began questioning what role she would have in her future husband's life. Would she be placed second to his relationship with Bob? She began putting pressure on Paul to distance himself from his brother Bob.

Paul was in love with his future bride, but he also loved and was very attached to his twin brother. Paul was fearful that if he were to marry, his wife would complain every time he saw Bob and make his life very unpleasant. Paul's response to his fiancée's pressure, however, was to withdraw and not deal with the situation. As the wedding day approached, he developed insomnia and panic attacks.

In therapy, Paul faced his dilemma, and realized that he needed to assert himself with his fiancée before the wedding. He spoke with her and made clear to her that if they were to marry she would come first. But she would have to accept the fact that his best friend, his twin brother, would continue to be an important part of his life. If she could not accept that, the wedding would be called off. He was not going to give up his relationship with his twin brother. His fiancée agreed, and the wedding went off as planned. Needless to say, his panic attacks and insomnia disappeared.

It's amazing if you think about it. The friendship of the identical twins Paul and Bob was so close that it jeopardized Paul's upcoming marriage. Those who know identical twins can attest to the closeness of their friendship. It's certainly much closer than that seen with fraternal twins or siblings near in age.

Treating Sandra and Paul and many other patients over the years has led me to the following model of friendship:

A PERSON WILL CHOOSE AS A FRIEND SOME-ONE WHO IS SIMILAR TO THEMSELVES. SOMEONE WITH A SIMILAR PERSONALITY, SENSE OF HUMOR, LEVEL AND TYPE OF INTELLIGENCE, INTERESTS, VALUES, LIKES, DISLIKES, ETC. AND THE CLOSER THE SIMILARITY, THE CLOSER THE FRIENDSHIP.

If we use a jigsaw puzzle model, we can say that *YOU WILL CHOOSE AS FRIENDS PEOPLE WHOSE JIGSAW PUZZLE PIECES RESEMBLE YOURS. AND THE MORE SIMILAR IN SHAPE A PUZZLE PIECE IS TO YOURS, THE CLOSER THE FRIENDSHIP.*

The following drawings illustrate this principle:

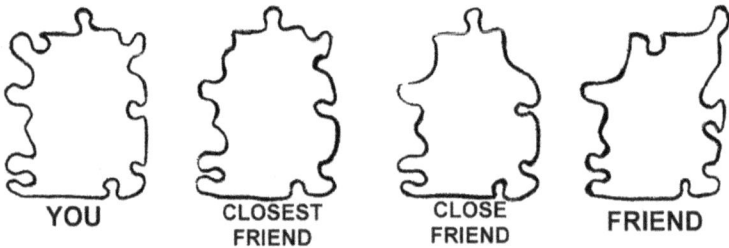

YOU CLOSEST FRIEND CLOSE FRIEND FRIEND

An important corollary to this model then is as follows: *If your friend's puzzle piece resembles yours, then your puzzle piece resembles your friend's. Thus, the friendship you have will be mutual—and to a similar degree of closeness.* That is, your friend will like your company, just as much as you like your friend's company.

Thus, if you know someone well, and on a scale of 1 to 10 you like that person a 6 or 7, you can predict that that individual will like you back a 6 or 7 as well. Not a 1 or a 10, but about a 6 or 7, which describes the degree your jigsaw puzzle pieces are similar.

The implication from this model is important. From our model it can be predicted that if you meet someone new, and you get to know that person well and you like that person a lot, you should not feel insecure that you will be rejected as a friend. That person will be receptive to your friendship. And ultimately will like you as much as a friend, as you like that person.

Thus, if you've observed someone you're attracted to as a possible friend, have the courage to go over and meet that person. The chances are excellent that a friendship will develop. In looking for friends, consequently, one should focus on finding people that you like, and not worry about being rejected. Again, the people whom you are attracted to as a possible friend will likely like you back as a friend— and equally as intensely.

A PERSONAL ANECDOTE:

I went to an out of town medical school where initially I knew no one in either my class or in the new city. We had 100 students in my freshman class. At first, I had a friendship with a group of 3 classmates. From my model of friendship, you could predict that they were fellows from my hometown of New York City. But although they were nice guys, my feelings toward them as friends were not very intense. If I gave it a number, I would say they were a 4 or 5 out of 10. However, not knowing anyone else well, and wanting some friends, I formed a friendship with guys who were frankly the best I could come up with. However, as the year progressed, I noticed another student in my class who didn't seem to have many friends. But there was something about him that I liked. He seemed rather low-key, he seemed considerate and respectful towards others, had a sense of humor, and he seemed to be sincerely interested in learning. He also came from the New York City area. I didn't know why exactly, but I felt that I would like him as a friend. And, intuitively, I felt that he would like me back as a friend.

One day, when I was standing in the school cafeteria lunch line, I noticed him eating by himself. And I said to myself, "When I get off this line, if he's still sitting there, I'm going to go over to his table and ask if I could sit with him. And I know that when I get up from that table, we'll be friends." And that's exactly what happened. He was my best friend throughout my four years in medical school, and made my medical school experience much more pleasant.

Looking back at this school experience, I realize that I was more similar to this medical student than I was to my initial friends. And I'm glad that I had the courage to go over to speak with him.

There may be times that you feel this model of friendship doesn't seem to work. That is, there may be a person you think you would like a lot as a friend, who doesn't seem to like you back that much. One has to keep in mind that it takes time for two people to get to know each other. However, *when two people know each other well, their degree of liking one another as friends—on a scale of 1 to 10—will be equal. If not equal at any one time, one or both individuals don't know each other well enough.*

If your overture toward friendship is not reciprocated by an individual, you should ask yourself whether your desire for a particular person as a friend is based solely upon who that person is, or whether it's based upon what that person can give you in addition to themselves. (Remember, our definition of friendship is liking someone for who that person is, and not for what that person can give you beyond themselves.) For example, you could like an individual and want that person to be your friend for the information that individual could provide you. Or you could like a person and want to be their friend because that individual is popular and could get you invited to parties where you could have fun and meet other people. Ultimately, if deep down you really only like a person a 6 or 7 out of 10, you can't expect that individual to like you back more than that.

Some people, in their desire to be popular and liked by individuals who are not truly destined to be their friend, will "sell" to these individuals. (See the chapter on "Buying and Not Selling.") You can sell, for example, by going very much out of your way to do these individuals favors. Or you can sell by being extremely and insincerely complimentary to them. There is nothing wrong with engaging in such behavior and being liked by people who are not truly meant to be your friends. But you should ask yourself, for what purpose? It requires an effort on your part, and at times, self-sacrifice. And if you're successful, what do you get for it? If you're an adult, you could wind up getting a dinner invitation from people you really don't want to spend any additional time with. Then what do you do, come up with excuses? As they say, be careful what you wish for—you may actually get it.

There are people whose self-esteem is based on their popularity; that is, the number of people who like them and want to be their friend. It's easy to get people to like you more than would be expected by the similarity of your jigsaw puzzle pieces, by giving them things in addition to yourself ("selling"). But the question you should ask yourself is, what happens when you stop giving? When you stop giving more than yourself, you'll find that their degree of liking you will fall back to the level that it was meant to be, based upon your similarity to each other. Meanwhile, you've spent a lot of time and effort in trying to achieve the goal of being liked. If you ultimately discover that these individuals are not that fond of you, realize that deep down you're really not that fond of them either. Don't take their not liking you that much, personally. (See the Chapter – "People will not like you that much—Don't take it Personally")

Of course, it's better to be liked than not liked. But unless you've done something to harm someone, there should be no reason why you should be disliked. To get people to like you, who are not truly destined to be a friend, requires an effort on your part. And you should ask yourself, why? And if there is a good objective reason … go for it!

AN ANECDOTE FROM MY PROFESSIONAL PRACTICE
My experience as a freshman in medical school in forming a close friendship was in marked contrast to the experience of a patient of mine. We'll call her Alice.

Alice was in her first year at a small out-of-town college. I saw her on spring break and she was very upset. It seemed that she had established a close friendship with two young girls at school. But it became apparent, after a while, that they preferred each other's company to that of Alice. For example, they would arrange to get together socially at times and did not include Alice. When Alice became aware of this, she became very angry. Her response was a defiant decision to not have anything more to do with these two young ladies. Even though they did not reject Alice as a friend—they just obviously preferred each other's company to that of Alice -*Alice would reject* **THEM.**

Though the price Alice paid for her defiance was increased loneliness at college, Alice was willing to pay this price because she was very proud. Alice interpreted her friends' preference for each other's company over hers as a statement that there was something "*less*" about her. In effect, Alice took her friends' preference for each other's company over hers very personally.

What was the flaw in Alice's thinking? And how SHOULD she have viewed her friends' preference for each other's company? If Alice had been aware of our jigsaw puzzle model of friendship, she could have interpreted her friends' actions differently and saved herself a lot of grief—and loneliness.

For example, keeping the jigsaw puzzle model of friendship in mind, Alice could have said to herself: *"These two young girls are more similar to each other than they are to me. That's why they prefer each other's company to that of mine. It doesn't mean that I am **LESS** than them—nor are they saying that. Perhaps if there were more young girls at this college, I could have found someone who would be more similar to me than she would be to my two friends. And she would have preferred **MY** company as a friend over **THEIRS**. But alas, it's a small college and we have what we have here. These two girls are the best I can come up with as friends. Better to have some friends than none. I'm **NOT** going to take their preference for each other's company over mine personally."*

The above corrected thinking for Alice illustrates cognitive therapy at work. That is, learning to process things in a way that is not only valid, but that can be helpful in functioning better. If Alice had kept the jigsaw puzzle model of friendship in mind, she would have been a happier college student.

AND THAT IS THE MAJOR POINT OF THIS BOOK: UNDERSTANDING AND KEEPING IN MIND THE JIGSAW PUZZLE MODELS OF RELATIONSHIPS IS NOT ONLY THEORETICALLY INTERESTING, BUT CAN BE HELPFUL IN FUNCTIONING BETTER. BUT A PERSON HAS TO KEEP THE MODELS IN MIND, AND PRACTICE APPLYING THEM IN THE VARIOUS SITUATIONS THAT ARE ENCOUNTERED IN LIFE FOR THEM TO BE HELPFUL. THE MORE THEY ARE PRACTICED, THE MORE HABITUAL THEY WILL BECOME TO A PERSON'S WAY OF THINKING, AND THE MORE HELPFUL THEY WILL BE.

BOTTOM LINE: The jigsaw puzzle model of a friendship is two jigsaw puzzle pieces that resemble each other. And the closer the resemblance, the closer the friendship. And the degree of liking each other as friends, when two people know each other well, will be equal.

FINDING FRIENDS THROUGH SUCCESSIVE APPROXIMATIONS

Mark was a 13-year-old young man whose father had recently been transferred to a job in New York City. Mark was feeling very lonely in New York City, having left all his friends behind in Ohio. How was he going to make new friends? He especially missed his best friend John.

If you're new to a town, finding new friends—or people whose company you enjoy—is not easy. But our jigsaw puzzle model of friendship gives us a template for finding friends and even a new best friend. How does this process work?

Remember that a friend will be someone who is similar to yourself. The more similar to yourself, the closer the friendship.

At school, Mark will be exposed to many individuals, some of whom he will like more, and some of whom he will like less. Those individuals he will like more are individuals who are more similar to himself, that is, those individuals whose jigsaw puzzle pieces most closely resemble his. He needs to have the courage to approach those individuals for friendship. According to our model of friendship, they should like him back to a similar degree as he likes them.

It's important to remember, however, that the people Mark initially meets as friends may only have a 6 or 7 out of 10 in degree of similarity to himself. Consequently, they may be only moderately receptive to his friendship. Mark needs to accept this as a natural phenomenon, and not take it personally. He has to keep in mind that he's not that wild about these individuals either—but that's the best he can come up with so far as he searches for friends. Ultimately, he will find closer friends.

However, if Mark manages to socialize with someone who is a 6 or 7 out of 10 in level of friendship, this individual will have a range of friends who will vary in their similarity to this initial friend; and perhaps Mark will find an individual or two that is more similar to himself than his initial friend. Maybe a level 7 or 8 out of 10.

And socializing with an individual who is a 7 or 8 out of 10 in similarity to Mark will expose Mark to this individual's friends who will also vary; and perhaps Mark will find someone in *this* group of friends who is an 8 or 9 out of 10 in similarity to Mark.

And so on and so forth, this process continues with Mark meeting through friends people he finds more and more similar to himself, until he finds someone who is **very** similar to himself. Perhaps someone as similar to himself as John, his best friend in Ohio. This person will then be his new best friend in the new town where he lives.

BOTTOM LINE: It takes time to find friends. Have the courage to approach and socialize with people you're somewhat attracted to as a possible friend. You may find that a friend's friend may be better suited to you as a friend than your initial friend. Repeating this process of socializing with *closer* friends will bring you to your *closest* friends.

PEOPLE ARE NOT
GOING TO LIKE YOU THAT MUCH—
DON'T TAKE IT PERSONALLY

Joan and her husband recently moved from a small town in South Carolina to New York City. In an effort to make new friends, Joan joined various organizations in New York. Joan was a friendly, outgoing person, and was very popular in South Carolina. But she found that her efforts to arrange get-togethers with some new acquaintances in New York, although responded to favorably initially, did not receive the follow-through she had hoped for. Joan was a very sensitive lady, and was very upset. "What's wrong with me," she said to her husband. "Why don't these women like me? What did I do wrong?"

At this point, it's important to remind ourselves of the jigsaw puzzle model of friendship: The jigsaw puzzle model of friendship dictates that people will want to be friends—or enjoy being in each other's company—to the degree they are similar to one another. That is, the degree people's puzzle pieces resemble each other's. **From our model it should follow then that people who are different from one another will not like each other that much.** *It doesn't mean these individuals will DISLIKE each other—it just means they won't like each other that much.* Joan, being from a small town in South Carolina, was very different than her new acquaintances in New York City. Many of these acquaintances probably already had close friends. And it's also understandable that they may not have been enthusiastic about the friendship of someone who may have been quite different than themselves.

Many people are similar to Joan, and take social rejection very personally. To treat these individuals and to decrease feelings of rejection, I ask these individuals to rate the people they meet on a scale of 1 to 10, based on their degree of liking the new people they encounter. The point of this exercise is to illustrate that if you only like someone a 5 or 6 out of 10, it should not come as a surprise, and it should be expected and accepted, when you discover that this individual only likes *you* a 5 or 6 out of 10 as well. In effect, your jigsaw puzzle pieces are quite different. Thus, not being liked that much should not be taken personally. Moreover, there is nothing much you can do about it unless you change who you are—or engage in "selling" behavior. (See the chapter on "Buying and Not Selling")

"Selling," of course, involves being nicer than you would normally choose to be for the purpose of getting an individual to like you. For example, going out of your way to do this individual a favor, or being extra complimentary to this individual. In doing so, perhaps this person's degree of liking you could rise to a level 7 or 8. But what happens when you remove these extra favors or compliments and are just being yourself? Well then, this person's degree of liking you would revert back to the 5 or 6 it was meant to be based upon your similarity—or the similarity of your jigsaw puzzle pieces.

Individuals rating their degree of liking the people they meet has additional benefits beyond diminishing sensitivity to rejection. This exercise (buying behavior), helps individuals become more in touch with their feelings and helps them become more proactive in their social encounters. In effect, it helps them practice "buying" behavior. It is a characteristic of people who strive to be liked to engage in conversation primarily focused on the reaction of the people they're speaking with, rather than focusing on what they themselves are feeling. This exercise helps individuals focus on how much they like the people they encounter, rather than on how much the people they encounter like **THEM**.

To determine how much you like the people you meet, you have to get to know them. This requires observing them and asking questions. To be blunt, it's like "examining the merchandise." Being proactive in observing and asking questions exposes the shapes of the puzzle pieces of the people you're speaking with, as well as indirectly exposing the shape of your own puzzle piece when you're asked similar questions back. This mutual exposure of puzzle pieces is an essential first step in finding people you like—and for people you like to find you.

Selling, or striving to be liked by people who inherently may not like you that much is problematic. Such behavior increases one's anxiety and lowers one's self esteem. It increases a person's anxiety by diminishing an individual's control in social encounters. The person you're speaking with is in control as you're focusing on pleasing that person, and what to say next to please that person—rather than focusing on what you really want to know. This type of interaction causes an individual to feel more anxious. It also lowers self-esteem by giving the other individual greater importance than yourself—which is registered by you unconsciously. When you treat yourself as if you're not worth that much, you will **FEEL** that you're not worth that much. And what you register unconsciously, the individuals you're speaking with register unconsciously as well. That is, when others feel that you don't hold yourself with much regard, they don't hold you with as much regard as well. As a result, they may not treat you with as much respect and consideration as they normally would—which further lowers your self-esteem. (This is not a deliberate action on the part of others—it's unconscious.) And when a person's self-esteem is lowered, unfortunately, it increases the tendency to "sell" all the more, because it reinforces a person's feeling that they're not worth very much. Thus, working to gain the acceptance and approval of others leads to a self-perpetuating cycle of anxiety and low self-esteem. It is not a good way of interacting.

The question should be asked, "Why do so many individuals work hard at being liked?" There are a number of possible reasons.

Probably the most common reason people strive to be liked is equating being liked with being a "good" person. This association is most likely connected to a religious upbringing. If you're a good Christian, you're taught to be generous and put other people first. And if you engage in this type of behavior, people will tend to like you more than they would otherwise. So, if you're not liked that much, perhaps you haven't been that good of a person, or not that good of a Christian. And we have to remember that America is primarily a Christian society.

Another possibility is that some people equate being liked with having more to offer objectively, or being a more valuable person. So, if you're not that popular, you're viewed as inferior to someone who is liked more. We saw an example of this type of thinking with Alice in the chapter on "Friendships."

Another reason for wanting to be liked is insecurity. That is, the more people who like you, the more likely you'll receive their help in time of need. Of course, these "friends" are not true friends based on our model of friendship. They have been bought by you by being overly kind, and will tend to disappear if you need them, as opposed to true friends who are more likely to help you in time of need.

And there are some individuals who want to be liked because they just can't tolerate being alone, and need many "friends."

BOTTOM LINE: Our jigsaw puzzle model of friendship dictates that people will like each other to the degree they are similar. Since you are different than other people, most people are not going to like you that much. It doesn't mean they will DISLIKE you, it just means they won't like you that much—which is actually the way you feel about them. So don't take it personally.

A ROMANTIC RELATIONSHIP

ave you ever wondered what causes an individual to choose one person as a romantic partner or spouse and not another? This question puzzled me for a long time. A patient of mine, Anne, provided me with what I felt was the answer to this question. Anne came to see me many years ago requesting hypnosis to lose weight. Anne was married, and in the course of treatment described how she met her husband, Michael.

Anne was sharing a summer house on Long Island; a community on Long Island where single people gather in the summertime to meet other single people. Anne shared her house with people with whom she was very comfortable—her sister, her cousin, and some friends.

People are very informal in this community, and often drop in and visit one another unannounced. Michael, a young man who lived nearby, visited Anne's house from time to time. Characteristically, when Michael would visit, Anne would be in the kitchen talking to the group at large, and then run out of the house to position herself next to some guy she had her eye on. Michael, however, began coming over more frequently, and the girls noticed while they were entertaining him that he would be focusing on Anne—not Anne's sister, her cousin, or her friends, but Anne. Anne, however, paid very little attention to Michael before running out of the house to try and meet someone she had her eye on. One day, the other young women in the house said to Anne, "Anne, you're looking for a boy-friend, and yet Michael seems to be interested in you and you don't pay any attention to him." And Anne said, "Who's Michael?" "You know," they said. "The guy who keeps coming by." "Oh," she said. "Him. He seems like a nice guy. I guess I could talk to him." "And, Dr. Almeleh," she said in session, "I spoke with Michael and in 10 minutes I knew that this was the guy, this was the guy I was going to marry." And she did.

I was intrigued by Anne's story. I asked myself, was it a coincidence that Anne felt this way about Michael? We knew that Michael was attracted to Anne. Was it a coincidence that Anne became attracted to Michael? The answer I came up with was, NO, it couldn't be a coincidence.

I thought that in this situation, where Anne was very comfortable, Anne's true personality was exposed for everyone in the house to see. And Michael, observing Anne, realized that Anne was the right person for him—not Anne's sister, her cousin, or her friends—just Anne. But Anne, not having spoken to Michael, was left only with her "fantasy," or her imagination of what Michael was like, based solely on a casual observation of his physical appearance. She didn't really *KNOW* Michael. (Or, by our model, she didn't know the true shape of his jigsaw puzzle piece.) But after she spoke with Michael and saw what he was like (or the true shape of his jigsaw puzzle piece), she realized that he was the right person for her. *Apparently, I thought, if it fits for one side, it's a fit for the other side.* Michael, having observed Anne as she really was—being herself, very comfortable among her friends—was the first of the two to see that Anne was right for him (or the right fit) as a romantic partner. But again, if it was right for Michael, it turned out to be right for Anne.

If I were to find a visual model of what seemed to have occurred with Anne and Michael, it was as if two jigsaw puzzle pieces seemed to have fit together. And if it fit for one side, it fit for the other side. Two jigsaw puzzle pieces fitting together would also represent graphically the common observation that in a romantic relationship "opposites attract." That is, opposite personality character traits create a sexual chemistry. But I felt that this graphic model would not represent a total accurate picture of a romantic relationship. Michael's attraction to Anne was more than sexual. He was also attracted to Anne as a person. How, I wondered, could I incorporate into a graphic model of a romantic relationship the important attribute that in a good, stable romantic relationship – and not just a purely sexual relationship—your romantic partner should also be a good friend?

From a previous chapter the model of a friendship I depicted was two jigsaw puzzle pieces that are very similar in their total overall shape**. Thus. the model I developed for a stable romantic relationship became illustrated as *TWO JIGSAW PUZZLE PIECES THAT FIT TOGETHER, OR ARE COMPLEMENTARY ON ONE SIDE OF THE PUZZLE PIECES, BUT ARE SIMILAR IN SHAPE ON THE SIDES OF THE PUZZLE PIECES THAT DON'T INTERLOCK.* Thus, the pair of puzzle pieces would have the characteristics of both a sexual attraction as well as a friendship.**

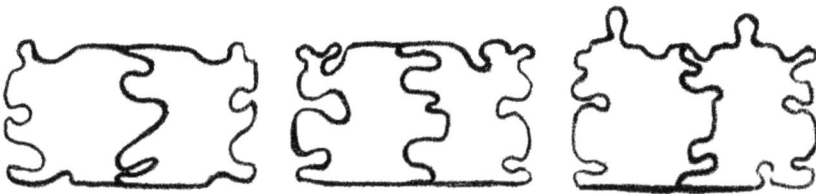

Again, in our model, the parts of the puzzle pieces (or characteristics of the two individuals) that are complementary— or opposite—are the aspects of the two individuals that create a sexual chemistry. And the parts of the puzzle pieces that are similar and don't interlock are the characteristics of the two individuals that are similar enough to create a friendship. You need both

elements for a good stable romantic relationship. (Illustration above)

Now, it's possible that you could have one without the other. That is, two people could have aspects of their personalities that are opposite, creating a sexual chemistry, but not enough characteristics that are similar to create a friendship. This relationship winds up being a sexual relationship, but not a long lasting, stable romantic relationship, because of the lack of a sufficient friendship component. Using our model, this relationship would be depicted as two puzzle pieces fitting together on one side of the puzzle pieces, but not very similar on the sides of the puzzle pieces that don't interlock.

Or it's possible that you could have a relationship in which too many characteristics of the two individuals are similar, and not enough that are opposite. In this case there are not enough opposite or complementary character traits to create a long term satisfying sexual relationship. With too many characteristics that are similar, and not enough that are opposite, a friendship rather than a romantic relationship would result. This would be depicted by puzzle pieces that are overall very similar in shape and consequently don't fit together, or complement each other, in many locations.

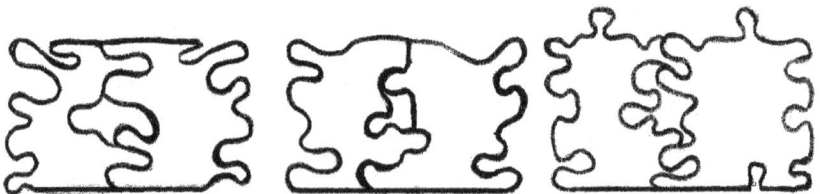

Using our jigsaw puzzle model, it's understandable that your ultimate choice of a life partner or spouse may be someone who didn't provide you with the most intense sexual experience you've ever had. It may be that the person who provided you with your most intense sexual experience was someone who was in **TOO** many ways opposite to you, and in not enough ways similar to you to enable a friendship. Ultimately you would want to enjoy spending time with your romantic partner outside the bedroom. This would not be the case where your romantic partner was someone where there were too many differences and not enough similarities for a close friendship to result.

The next question you may ask is, what are the complementary character traits in a romantic relationship that create a sexual chemistry? And what are the similar character traits that create a friendship?

Some of the opposite or complementary character traits that are seen in a romantic relationship are:

1. Focused vs. Distractible: Obsessive, organized, and focused individuals are sexually attracted to artistic, creative, and more distractible individuals—and vice versa. For example, a lawyer or accountant type of person would be sexually attracted to an interior designer or an artistic type of person who is more "flighty," or associative in their thinking pattern.

2. Extroverted vs. Introverted: Outgoing people are sexually attracted to people who are more shy and reserved—and vice versa.

3. More self-absorbed vs. More focused on others: Self-absorbed and very self-serving individuals are sexually attracted to people who are more aware and responsive to other people's needs—and vice versa.

4. Assertive vs. Unassertive: People who are assertive and have no problem going after what they want are sexually attracted to individuals who are more reserved about asking for, and getting what they want—and vice versa.

The above list is not meant to be exhaustive. The point is that opposite personality character traits are necessary to create a sexual chemistry. And the sexual attraction is mutual.

And the character traits that if shared, that enable a friendship—and thus the maximum chance for success for a long-lasting romantic relationship – are as follows:

1. Similar levels of intelligence: Even though the types of intelligence may differ (for example, mathematical or scientific type of intelligence vs. artistic intelligence), the most successful relationships are with those individuals who share the same *degree* or *level* of intelligence.

2. Similar sense of humor – similar in both the *extent* that humor is appreciated, and the *type* of humor that is appreciated.

3. Similar values and interests.

4. Similar cultural and religious backgrounds.

Although couples lacking some of these similarities, or elements of a friendship, can and do form romantic relationships, couples with these similarities seem to achieve the greatest satisfaction in their romantic relationships. And their romantic relationships seem to be the most stable.

BOTTOM LINE: The jigsaw puzzle model of a stable romantic relationship is two jigsaw puzzle pieces that fit together or complement each other along one side of the puzzle pieces, and are similar to each other on the sides of the puzzle pieces that don't interlock. The parts of the puzzle pieces that interlock represent personality character traits of the two individuals that are opposite and create a sexual chemistry. And the sides of the puzzle pieces that don't interlock but are similar in shape represent the characteristics of the two individuals that are similar and enable a close friendship. The presence of *both* of these components are necessary to create the most stable, long-lasting romantic relationships.

It thus follows from our model of a stable romantic relationship that *if you know a person well*, and you feel that that individual is right for you, then you are right for that individual. Stated simply, if it "fits" for one side, it "fits" for the other side.

GAY OR STRAIGHT—
THE MODELS ARE THE SAME

*T*his is an important point: **THE JIGSAW PUZZLE MODELS OF RELATIONSHIPS—BOTH FOR FRIENDSHIPS AND ROMANTIC RELATIONSHIP—ARE THE SAME FOR BOTH GAY AND STRAIGHT INDIVIDUALS.**

But there is a characteristic of gay male *sexual* relationships that causes it to differ somewhat from straight sexual relationships. And that is that there are two men involved in the sexual activity, rather than a man and a woman.

If we hypothesize that men, due to genetic factors, are inherently more sexually driven than women, we would expect to see more frequent sexual activity among gay male couples compared to straight couples. With more eagerly and readily available consensual partners, gay men have the ability to engage in more frequent sexual activity compared to straight men, who have to rely on consensual females for their sexual relations. And this higher sex drive for the male human animal seems to be true for a variety of animal species.

HOWEVER, despite this apparent increased tendency for sexual behavior among gay men, it needs to be emphasized that in a gay romantic relationship, the same factors determine the choice of a life partner and the stability of a romantic relationship as in a straight relationship. It is important to remember that a romantic attachment is primarily an emotional attachment. And it doesn't matter whether the individual is straight or gay.

BOTTOM LINE: The jigsaw puzzle model for both friendship and a romantic relationship is the same for both gay and straight individuals.

"BUYING" AND NOT "SELLING"

This is a concept and an approach to meeting new people that patients have found extremely helpful in finding friendships or a possible romantic relationship.

Whether looking for friends or romance (or just meeting new people in general), "buying" refers to approaching the people you meet as if they were merchandise you were evaluating to see how much you like them. In evaluating any product (or person), you have certain questions in mind. Specifically, as it relates to a person, where does this person live? What does this person do? What are this person's interests? etc. Buying is being in touch with your feelings and asking the questions you would like to have answered. It's a proactive, assertive approach to meeting new people. And there's nothing wrong with this approach when it's done in a polite fashion. In buying, the true shape of the jigsaw puzzle piece of the person you're speaking with is revealed. Thus, buying helps you figure out whether you want to see this person again, as either a potential friend or romantic partner.

Unfortunately, too often people approach the meeting of new people in "selling" mode. "Selling" is the opposite of buying. In selling, you're focused on trying to get the person you're speaking with to like you, rather than trying to figure out how much you like this individual. Selling is not a good approach for a number of reasons.

In selling, the true shape of the other person's jigsaw puzzle piece is not revealed, because you're too busy selling yourself and not asking the questions you would like answered, and need to have answered to know what the other person is like. If the shape of the other person's puzzle piece is not revealed, how will you know to what degree you like this individual and whether you want to see this person again? If you're looking for a friend or a romantic relationship, it's not the most efficient way to find someone. In fact, it could be counterproductive.

Witness the old adage, "Be careful what you wish for, you may actually get it." In selling yourself, as you attempt to please and be accepted by others, the shape of your own jigsaw puzzle piece as seen by others is distorted. The person these people see is not the real you. And the people you meet may actually *like* what they see, and want to see you again. But you may not want to see *them* again. Now you're faced with the difficult situation of either having to come up with excuses why you can't meet, or having to accept, for example, a dinner invitation with individuals you have no desire to spend any additional time with.

In addition to leading to relationships that may not be well-suited for you, selling can present other problems. For example, selling often results in boring conversations. If you're not going to ask personal questions to the person you're speaking with, this person has a tendency to not ask personal questions back. You both may wind up discussing things neither of you has much interest in—such as the weather. Many people refer to these conversations as "small talk," which most people find boring.

People who are in the habit of selling often feel that people find them boring. And they're probably correct. People probably *do* find them boring. To diminish being boring *and* bored, you need to be a buyer.

When a person engages in a conversation in buying mode by asking personal questions, it often leads the individual you're speaking with to ask similar personal questions back. As a result, both people reveal themselves to each other. And according to our theory, you're more likely to find satisfying friendships and romantic relationships by each person revealing the true shape

of their jigsaw puzzle piece. And an important side effect of this approach is that both people are not bored because they're asking the questions they're interested in knowing the answers to.

I often make the analogy that good conversation should be similar to good sex. Each person is assertively going after what he or she wants, with the other individual ultimately in control of allowing or not allowing what is requested. When this is not the case, and an individual is primarily focused on pleasing the other person, it often does not work out well. In fact, in this situation men will often lose their erection.

Selling also has the detrimental effect of increasing a person's anxiety while engaged in conversation. Focusing on what to say next to please the other person, rather than on what you really want to know, causes anxiety and creates a feeling of being less in control. A person is less in control because your conversation is guided by the reaction of the other person. Selling can wind up being very tiring and feeling like a lot of work. Consequently, people who sell tend to dread the very thing they need to do if they're trying to find and establish new relationships—that is, meet new people. And the more a person sells, the more anxious a person will be in their conversations.

The question is, what causes an individual to engage in selling behavior as opposed to buying behavior? There are a number of possible reasons.

Some people feel that buying behavior is impolite. They feel that asking personal questions puts an individual, who may not feel comfortable revealing themselves, "on the spot." However, it should be kept in mind that no one is *forcing* an individual to answer a question, and people can be evasive if they choose to be. I do think, however, it would be impolite to pursue a line of questioning if the person shows obvious discomfort or resistance in answering. But there is nothing wrong with asking questions.

Buying is ultimately an example of **assertive** behavior—that is, asking for something you want—such as information. Assertive behavior should be distinguished from **aggressive** behavior—which is *forcing* an individual to give something they don't want to give. As long as an individual is in control to either answer or not, there is nothing wrong with being assertive and asking for the information you would like to know. I'm sure a person's good taste would stop an individual from asking questions that most people would feel are *too* personal. However, *even then,* asking such a question is still an example of assertive behavior because the individual asked is not forced to answer the question.

A person may have a tendency to engage in selling rather than buying behavior when they are uncomfortable exposing themselves. An individual may realize subconsciously that asking personal questions often leads to being asked similar personal questions back. And perhaps that individual is not comfortable with exposing, for example, what kind of job they have, or where they live—that is, revealing their socio-economic status. This person may wind up engaging in "small talk" to avoid being asked these personal questions, even though this individual may very well want to know the answer to these questions from the person they're speaking with.

Selling can also originate from a person's low self-esteem, and a consequent desire to be liked and accepted by others. And when selling results from low self-esteem (as discussed in a previous chapter), it unfortunately perpetuates low self-esteem and continued selling behavior. That is, it becomes a vicious cycle. Selling is saying to yourself and to the people around you that they have greater importance than you, and that your job is to please them, take care of them and entertain them. And if the people you're speaking with are aware of this, even unconsciously, they will view you in a diminished fashion and treat you—most likely, unintentionally—with less deference. When you treat yourself as having less worth, people will view you as having less worth. This unfortunately reinforces your feeling of low self-esteem and continued selling behavior.

Unlike selling behavior, engaging in conversation in buying mode tends to have the opposite effect. It *raises* one's self-esteem. And it creates a self-perpetuating cycle of increased self-esteem. Buying behavior shows to yourself and others that you value yourself to the extent that you're taking care of your needs, by, for example, asking questions you want to have answered. When you treat yourself as having significant worth, others view you as having significant worth and treat you accordingly. This reinforces the feelings of positive regard you have for yourself, and continued buying behavior.

Thus, unless you're running for office or have something you really want to sell to people—like a tangible product—there's really no point in selling. If your goal is to find good friendships and satisfying romantic relationships, buying is the approach you should take. Selling is inefficient, counterproductive, anxiety-generating, and can lower your self-esteem.

People who have been in the habit of selling most of their lives often feel that they'll have a hard time changing. And they're somewhat correct. Selling is an automatic response these individuals have as soon as they enter a social situation. **But automatic responses can be changed.** It just requires practice. **In social situations, what can be helpful is to repeat the mantra to yourself—"I'M BUYING ……... I'M NOT SELLING."** This mantra will remind you of the mental approach you *should* be taking, and help you to focus on being a buyer. When you find yourself slipping back into selling mode—as will happen—just repeat the mantra to yourself. It will switch you back into buying mode. Although this approach may seem simplistic, it has worked for many of my patients. Try it. Eventually you'll find that the buying approach will become your predominant response, or way of thinking when you're in social gatherings. And you'll discover that you're less anxious during conversations, and your self-esteem will rise.

The above is an example of cognitive therapy at work—practicing an exercise to change the way you think and react in a situation so that you can function better. And functioning better, and getting your needs met in terms of personal relationships, are the major goals of this book.

BOTTOM LINE: "Buying" exposes the true shape of someone's jigsaw puzzle piece, and ultimately the shape of one's own jigsaw puzzle piece, and makes easier the finding of satisfying friendships and romantic relationships. "Selling" is the opposite. Selling distorts the shape of one's own jigsaw puzzle piece, creates anxiety in social situations, may get you into relationships that are not right for you, and is a waste of time. Unless there is a product you really want to sell... be a buyer.

BEING VERY PHYSICALLY ATTRACTIVE

Sarah was a woman I treated many years ago for depression. She was extremely overweight and most people would say facially, she was not very attractive. After Sarah's depression lifted, she asked if I would treat her husband, Don, who was having some work-related difficulties. I agreed. At the scheduled appointment time, I went to the waiting room I shared to look for Don, but at first glance did not see him. Suddenly a very handsome gentleman asked, "Are you looking for me?" I have to admit, I was stunned. He was not what I had expected. I expected someone not very physically attractive, like Sarah.

In the course of Don's treatment, I was curious how they met.

Sarah was an attorney who also had an interest in theatre and the arts, and Don was a very successful actor. Sarah, in an effort to satisfy her interest in the arts, taught a course in law and the arts at an alternative school in Manhattan, in which Don had enrolled. During the series of lectures, Don noticed that there was something about Sarah's personality that he liked. At first, he admitted, he did not find Sarah physically attractive. He would stay after class, however, and speak with her. Eventually, they went out after class socially. After continuing to spend time together, Don noticed an emotional attachment developing towards Sarah, followed later by a sexual interest. When I saw them in treatment, they had been happily married for many years.

Sarah and Don, and other patients I have treated over the years, taught me something very important. ***PHYSICAL BEAUTY IS NOT ONE OF THE COMPONENTS OF ONE'S JIGSAW***

**PUZZLE PIECE THAT FACTORS INTO A STABLE RO-
MANTIC RELATIONSHIP.** Physical beauty can get a person to
first base, so to speak, but it is not one of the components that creates
a bond in a long-term romantic relationship. In fact, with some individuals, it can actually work against them. Take the case of my patient,
Sheryl.

Sheryl was a beautiful blond young lady, who came to
see me because she was very depressed. Although Sheryl was
very beautiful, and would get a lot of attention and sexual
"hook-ups," none of the men stuck around long enough to
give her the permanent relationship she craved.

Sheryl, unfortunately, had very low self-esteem. No
doubt because of the way she was treated by her father—a gentleman who constantly put her down while she was growing
up. As an adult, Sheryl looked at the attention she received
from men, especially if they were attractive and successful, as
verification of her worth—which raised her self-esteem. Consequently, Sheryl placed high hopes on relationships that were
really not well-suited for her. They were not the right match
and fit for her jigsaw puzzle piece.

In her relationships, Sheryl was a "seller" rather than a
"buyer." Although one would have expected Sheryl's good
looks to easily enable her to be a buyer, such was not the case.
Her low self-esteem caused her to search for acceptance, and
be a seller. And, unfortunately, she had many eager men, not
right for her, very interested in what she was selling.

Because of Sheryl's very low self-esteem, she took any
rejection from the men she had had a short relationship with,
very personally. "What's wrong with me?" she would ask.
"There are so many girls out there that are not as pretty as I
am that have steady boyfriends; I must *really* be a loser." There
were many sessions that Sheryl came in after a liaison that

didn't work out feeling so seriously depressed, that I considered hospitalizing her.

In treatment, I tried to counteract the negative feedback Sheryl got from her father by having her focus on her many very positive character traits. I also tried to have her internalize the concept of the jigsaw puzzle model of a romantic relationship, and realize that the right puzzle piece for her would be based on factors other than her good looks. And that she had to use her good looks to be a "buyer" —taking advantage of the attention she received to "examine the merchandise" and see who was right for her. But like many "sellers," especially with low self-esteem, it was hard for her to have the courage to let go, be herself, and be a buyer. Her good looks actually worked against her, in that she received interest from men too easily. She was too afraid at that point to be herself and possibly lose the interest she had already gotten without much effort. Men were very attracted to her, and she was afraid that she would turn them off by being herself. Unfortunately, she went for immediate gratification. But the gratification didn't last very long.

Despite Sheryl's physical beauty, Sheryl was one of the most challenging patients I have ever treated. Good looks can be a help in finding a romantic relationship—*if it's combined with being a buyer*. But it can also work against you if you're a seller, and you take the many rejections you're bound to receive, personally.

When women who are not as physically attractive as Sheryl receive attention, they receive attention with less emphasis paid to their looks, and more emphasis paid to other factors such as personality, etc., that **ARE** the determinants for the right fit and match for a successful romantic relationship. In that sense, these less attractive women were better off than Sheryl.

There is no doubt that overall being very physically attractive can be a plus in establishing a romantic relationship. It will get many people to take a step closer to "look over the merchandise," so to speak. And as will be mentioned in the next chapter, to find satisfying relationships you have to be "in it to win it." And there are few things that will get you more "in it" than being very physically attractive. But you have to combine being very physically attractive with being a buyer. Otherwise, it could work against you.

BOTTOM LINE: Physical beauty will cause people to take a step closer to "look over the merchandise," but it is **NOT** one of the characteristics, or facets, of a puzzle piece that creates a stable romantic relationship.

HOW TO FIND FRIENDS OR
A ROMANTIC RELATIONSHIP

Understanding the jigsaw puzzle model of both a friendship and a romantic relationship can provide a pathway to finding satisfying relationships. This chapter elaborates on that pathway.

YOU'VE GOT TO BE IN IT TO WIN IT: If you stay at home, your chances of finding a friend or romantic partner is practically nonexistent (unless you're visited by many traveling salespeople) ☺ . You've got to be out in the world, involved in life.

BE WHO YOU ARE: To find a person that's right for you as a friend or romantic partner requires exposing the shape of your jigsaw puzzle piece for the world around you to see. If you do this, after observing you, the people that are right for you as a friend or romantic partner will have a tendency to take a step forward and approach you. And the people who are not right for you can take a step back. You have to understand, expect, and accept that the vast majority of people are not right for you, and consequently may take a step back. You need to feel that that's okay (and perhaps even welcomed). The people who could create a significant difference in making your life happier and more fulfilled as either a friend or romantic partner will have the opportunity to see you and take a step forward. And one does not need many close relationships to lead a much happier and fulfilled life.

DO THINGS YOU LIKE TO DO: For both a friendship and a romantic relationship, you need people who are somewhat similar to you. If you do things you like doing, you have a greater chance of meeting people with similar interests, values, etc.

MEET PEOPLE THROUGH FRIENDS: Meeting people through friends is probably the easiest and best way to find people who could make a significant difference in your life, either as a friend or romantic interest.

Finding Friends: Finding friends through friends is discussed in the Chapter "Finding Friends through Successive Approximations."

Finding a Romantic Interest: If your friend has a romantic partner (whose puzzle piece consequently fits and matches yours to a slight degree as well), there is a better than random chance that the friends of your friend's romantic partner will be individuals that may fit and match your puzzle piece to a significant degree. Meeting people through the friends of a friend's romantic partner certainly has a greater potential for success in finding a romantic relationship than meeting people randomly through your general exposure to people.

BE A BUYER: In addition to being yourself and exposing the shape of your jigsaw puzzle piece so that the right people can approach you, you should try to expose the shape of the puzzle pieces of the people you meet. That way, you can see if there are people around you that *you* would like as a friend or romantic partner. In this book, we refer to this as being a "buyer" —or "examining the merchandise." (See the Chapter on "Buying and Not Selling.")

IF YOU ARE VERY DIFFERENT THAN THE NORM, YOU MAY HAVE MORE DIFFICULTY FINDING FRIENDS OR A ROMANTIC RELATIONSHIP. DON'T GIVE UP. AND DON'T TAKE IT PERSONALLY: Since an element of both a friendship and a stable romantic relationship is commonality, or being somewhat similar, someone who is unusual may have more difficulty finding satisfying relationships. For example, someone who is much smarter than the average person would need friends and a romantic partner that would be much smarter than the average individual as well. Since most people are of average intelligence, people who are much smarter than the average will have a much smaller population from which to find people that are right for them as either a friend or a romantic interest.

People from a minority cultural or religious background would also have more difficulty finding satisfying relationships, because by definition, people with those characteristics are in a minority.

Since many colleges select students of a similar scholastic achievement, colleges provide an opportunity for students of similar levels of intelligence to meet each other. Similarly, religious and minority cultural organizations often have socials for young people to meet.

I often illustrate the difficulty for someone who is very bright, for example, to find satisfying relationships by what is referred to as a "bell-shaped curve." This graph demonstrates the number of people at each level of intelligence by the space under a particular point on the curve. The larger the space under that particular point on the curve, the more people available at that level of intelligence. The "tail ends" of the curve—or both ends of the curve—with a much smaller space under those parts of the curve depict the fewer people available at these extreme levels of intelligence. (Illustration)

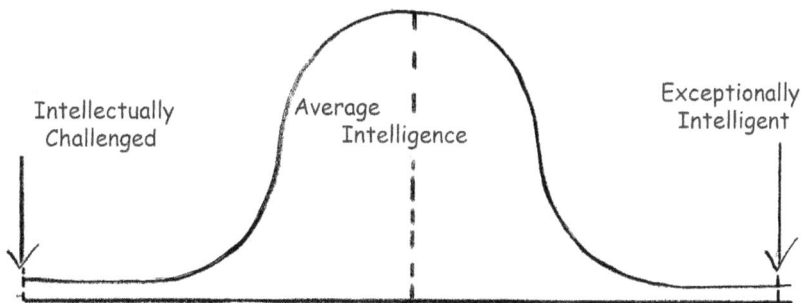

41

You can see from the graph that the space under the right tail end of the curve is much smaller than the space under the middle of the curve. That is, people who are much smarter than the average will have fewer people from whom to choose to find a satisfying friendship or romantic relationship, compared to people who are in the middle of the curve, or people of average intelligence. What this means is that if a very bright person goes to the routine singles bar to meet someone, this person will most likely be very frustrated, because he or she will have fewer appropriate matches from whom to choose, since most people will be of average intelligence. This graph can be very helpful for people who are very bright and somehow take personally their frustration in finding satisfying relationships. It illustrates the reason for their frustration, and may also illustrate their need to find a different venue than the one they have been using to find a romantic interest, or friends.

NEVER PUT ANYONE DOWN YOU DISCOVER IS NOT RIGHT FOR YOU: This is an important point. Being critical of others who are different than you, and consequently not right for you as a friend or romantic partner, is not a good thing for you to do. First of all, people around you who hear your criticism will feel someday you could do the same to them and may feel anxious getting close to you. Secondly, if you habitually criticize others (even in your mind, without saying it), you will feel, on some level, that others whom you meet for the first time could have the tendency to do the same to you. And this could cause you to be "gun shy" in meeting new people—which is counterproductive in making new friends or finding a potential romantic interest. Besides, it is not a nice thing to do. (This is the one judgment I will make in this book.) The subject of being critical of others is covered more extensively in a later chapter.

BOTTOM LINE: Finding friends or a satisfying romantic relationship requires some work. But the jigsaw puzzle model of relationships provides a pathway for achieving these goals.

BEING REJECTED
IN A ROMANTIC RELATIONSHIP

Being rejected in a romantic relationship is emotionally difficult. But keeping in mind the jigsaw puzzle model of a romantic relationship should make it easier to accept the rejection and move on. How so?

As a review—the jigsaw puzzle model of a successful romantic relationship is two jigsaw puzzle pieces that fit together (or complement each other) on one side of the puzzle pieces, and are similar in shape on the sides of the puzzle pieces that don't interlock.

The characteristics of the individuals that are opposite create the sexual attraction that exists between the two people—and the characteristics that are similar create the friendship components that are necessary for a long-term successful romantic relationship.

There is an important implication in this model of a romantic relationship: **When two people know each other well, the degree of romantic attachment each has for the other will be equal.** That is, if an individual knows his or her partner well, and feels it is a good *fit* (opposite characteristics, creating a sexual chemistry), and *match* (similar characteristics creating a friendship) for that individual, our model indicates that it should be a good fit and match for their partner. To make things easier, we denote this by saying: *"If it fits for one side, it fits for the other side."* (Here the word "fit" is used to describe puzzle pieces having *both* opposite and similar characteristics.) Moreover, our theory states that the **DEGREE** of the fit and match will be equal for both parties. Thus it follows that: ***If it's NOT a very good fit and match for one puzzle piece, then it should not be, and will not be, a very good fit and match for the other.***

You'll notice that this model of a romantic relationship does not find fault with any one individual when a romantic relationship doesn't work or fit. There is no good or bad value ascribed to any one individual in an unsuccessful romantic relationship. It's just that the two people were not right for each other, or not the right fit and match.

At times, however, this theory of an equality in the degree of a romantic attachment for the two parties may not seem to hold. That is, a person could feel a strong romantic attachment to an individual that is not reciprocated at all, or not reciprocated in equal intensity. Thus, a person could be rejected romantically, even though the rejected individual felt that a strong "fit," certainly on their part, was there. They may ask, "How come the other person didn't feel what I felt? What went wrong?" There are a number of possible explanations:

YOU REALLY DIDN'T KNOW YOUR ROMANTIC PARTNER WELL: It takes time to get to know someone well. Or, using the analogy of a deck of cards—it takes time for an individual to show all the cards in their hand. If you're a buyer (see the chapter on "Buying and not Selling"), and ask questions, both of you are more likely to get to know each other well, in a shorter period of time. However, if you're not a buyer—for whatever reason as was discussed in that chapter—then it will take much longer to get to know each other well. In the latter case you may have fallen in love with a fantasy—that is your *imagination* of what the other person was like—rather than the reality of who that person really was. Thus, the individual doing the rejecting may have seen the reality first—that is, that the "fit" wasn't there—and rejected you.

What you should say to yourself in rejections such as this, is: "I have to trust this person's judgment. If this individual saw that we were not the right fit and match for each other, then I would have ultimately seen the same thing, and felt the same way. This person just saw it before I did. If I wasn't the right "fit" for that person, then that person wasn't the right "fit" for me. Let me find someone with whom I **AM** the right fit."

IF YOU'RE MORE OUTGOING, YOU'RE MORE LIKELY TO BE REJECTED. (DON'T TAKE IT PERSONALLY): If you're a very outgoing or expressive individual, you'll more rapidly expose yourself or show the true shape of your jigsaw puzzle piece, before the other individual has had an equal chance to do so. Thus, if you're not the right "fit," your quieter and less expressive partner will be the first to see it, and reject you.

As alluded to briefly before, I often use the model of a deck of cards. Everyone's jigsaw puzzle piece can be represented by a specific hand of cards. And in a romantic relationship there is a hand of cards out there that would be the right hand for you. The right fit and match. When you see someone at a distance, for example at a cocktail party, you may see a few cards in that individual's hand that seem to be part of the ideal hand of cards for you. People then often fantasize or imagine that the rest of the cards in that individual's hand are the right ones for you as well. However, when you speak to that individual, the rest of that individual's cards are put down slowly. If you're more outgoing, you will have put down more cards in a given period of time than the other individual has. Consequently, the other person will be in a much better position to see, before you do, if you're not the right hand for that individual. But if you're not the right hand for that individual, then that individual is also not the right hand for you. And in this case, when rejected, you should say to yourself something similar to what was stated in the previous example:

"This person saw before I did that we're not the right fit and match for each other. That's okay. If I had gotten to know this person better, I would have seen the same thing. This person just saw it before I did. If I'm not the right fit and match for this individual, then this individual is not the right fit and match for me. And it's better to know sooner rather than later. I'm going to continue being myself and find the person that *IS* right for me."

IF YOU'RE DESPERATE FOR A RELATIONSHIP, YOU'RE MORE LIKELY TO TRY AND FIT A RELATIONSHIP THAT IS NOT RIGHT FOR YOU: Sometimes a person is so eager for a romantic relationship that they are willing to settle for a relationship that's not the best fit and match. In the courtship phase of a relationship they may even try to hide, subconsciously, who they really are for fear of "turning off" the other individual. This behavior, however, does not stop the other individual from ultimately discovering if the fit and match is right for that person. And if it is not the right fit, you will ultimately be rejected.

IF YOU'RE A VERY PHYSICALLY ATTRACTIVE PERSON, BE PREPARED FOR VERY FRUSTRATING ROMANTIC EXPERIENCES. ALTHOUGH YOU WILL HAVE MORE OPPORTUNITIES FOR SUCCESS, YOU WILL ALSO HAVE MORE DISAPPOINTMENTS THAN THE AVERAGE INDIVIDUAL: As discussed in the chapter "Being very Physically Attractive," if you're a physically attractive person, people will show greater interest in you. They may try to "sell" to you because of their sexual interest. That is, they will try to say what they think you would like to hear in order to have a romantic relationship with you, even if they themselves don't realize they're doing so. Ultimately, however, perhaps after a number of dates or sexual encounters, you're likely to be rejected if, and when, the individual realizes that you're not the right fit and match for that person. Remember that a romantic relationship is primarily a mental and emotional relationship. Sex is secondary.

It is important to keep in mind that good looks is *not* one of the characteristics that determine the right fit and match in a romantic relationship. To avoid this frustration, if you're very physically attractive you have to be a "buyer" in your approach to romantic relationships. (See the chapter on "Buying and not Selling.") You will have to screen the individuals who are showing an interest in you, and weed out those who are not right for you. If you're not a "buyer" in your approach to people, you're going to have problems. You'll be frequently disappointed. But you shouldn't take personally the frequent rejections that you will receive in romantic relationships. *Although you will have more disappointments, you will also have more opportunities for success than a less attractive person—IF YOU'RE A "BUYER."*

IF YOU'RE RICH OR FAMOUS—AS WITH INDIVIDU-ALS WHO ARE VERY PHYSICALLY ATTRACTIVE—YOU'LL BE IN FOR MANY DISAPPOINTMENTS: As with those individuals who are very physically attractive, being rich or famous presents more opportunities for success, but also more disappointments in finding the right romantic attachment. And more work—as people will try to "sell" to you if you're considered a very desirable "catch." You'll have to be a "buyer" and see who is right for you, even though your romantic partner may be selling. And by our model, if you determine that someone is right for you—then you're right for that person. Otherwise, relationships will fall apart when the novelty of a romantic involvement with a rich or famous person wears thin. What is then left are real people where the fit and match may not be there. As is the case with good looks, a long-term satisfying romantic relationship does not depend on money or fame, but the other characteristics as discussed in the chapter on "A Romantic Relationship."

Thus, if you're rich or famous, you have no choice but to be a buyer, if you're looking for a stable, satisfying romantic involvement. When you have examined the "merchandise" well, and you feel that an individual is right for you, our romantic model states that you are right for that individual—and the relationship will be stable. Often rich and famous people get flattered and seduced into unstable romantic relationships by people who are sellers.

IF YOU'RE "STRAIGHT" IN YOUR SEXUAL ORIENTATION AND DEVELOP A ROMANTIC ATTACHMENT TO SOMEONE WHO IS GAY, BE PREPARED TO BE DISAPPOINTED AND ULTIMATELY MOST LIKELY REJECTED. THE JIGSAW PUZZLE MODEL OF A ROMANTIC RELATIONSHIP DOES NOT APPLY TO A ROMANTIC RELATIONSHIP OF A STRAIGHT INDIVIDUAL WITH A GAY INDIVIDUAL: Using our romantic model, even if you know the other individual well and their jigsaw puzzle piece is the right fit and match for you, one crucial element is missing for the gay individual—you're not the right gender. It's bound to be very frustrating and disappointing. And ultimately, you'll most likely be rejected. My advice to you is to move on.

In my experience as a psychiatrist, I have treated many women who were married to gay men who were "in the closet." Almost invariably, these women noticed something was missing in their relationship. They didn't notice the emotional intensity or jealousy that they would have expected from a spouse. These women frequently asked their spouse for reassurance that they were loved. Their feelings were of course understandable. There **WAS** something missing. They were not the right gender for their romantic partner. They would have had a more stable and intensely emotional relationship with someone who was straight.

BOTTOM LINE: Keeping the jigsaw puzzle model of a romantic relationship in mind should make it easier to accept rejection from a romantic interest. If a romantic relationship is not a good fit and match for one individual, it will not be a good fit and match for the other. One person may discover this before the other and do the rejecting, but eventually the rejected individual would have made the same discovery and taken the same step.

BEING TOO NICE IS NOT GOOD

There are people who repeatedly form romantic attachments with individuals who are very selfish. Unfortunately, in our society this pattern is more commonly seen in women. The result most often is a very frustrating and unhappy romantic relationship. A patient of mine, Joanne, illustrated this.

Joanne came into treatment depressed and very angry. She discovered that the boyfriend she had dated for over a year—*and was financially supporting*—was cheating on her. "He was very generous and attentive when we first met," she said, "but soon after he moved in with me, he stopped working and I wound up paying all the bills. He was even brazen enough to use the cell phone I paid for, to carry on his affair. What's wrong with me?" she said. "Why do I keep falling for these types of guys? *And how do they find me?*"

Joanne, a very sweet, soft-spoken young lady went on: "I sit next to this woman at work who is such a bitch. Not only is she not nice to me, but she's not nice to everyone around her. And on Valentine's Day she's sitting there with a dozen roses on her desk from her boyfriend, while I'm sitting there staring at my boyfriend's cell phone bill, *with charges to his girl-friend. How do I find these guys?*"

Joanne went on to explain that this has been the typical experience she has had dating men. Things start off well in the courting phase of their romantic relationship, but soon afterwards things start to deteriorate and she finds that she's giving a great deal and they're giving very little. Ultimately, she winds up frustrated and unhappy, and breaks up the relationship, only to repeat this pattern in her next romantic attachment.

The question that needs to be asked is, "Why does this pattern repeat itself in Joanne's romantic life?" And more importantly, "What can be done to change this pattern so that the next man Joanne falls for winds up being a nicer and more generous person?"

To answer these questions, it may be helpful to review our model of a romantic relationship: The jigsaw puzzle model of a stable romantic relationship is two jigsaw puzzle pieces that complement each other, or fit together along one side of the puzzle pieces—but are similar in shape on the sides of the puzzle pieces that don't interlock. The parts of the puzzle pieces that fit or lock together represent the characteristics of the two individuals that are opposite and create the sexual chemistry that exists between two individuals. (The old adage "opposites attract" applies here.) And the parts of the puzzle pieces that don't interlock, and are similar, correspond to the characteristics of the two individuals that are similar and create the friendship that should exist in a long-term satisfying romantic relationship. Thus, the ideal romantic relationship are two jigsaw puzzle pieces that are opposite in shape along one side of the puzzle pieces that interlock and are similar in shape along the sides of the puzzle pieces that don't interlock.

But here is the important point: It is an observation that one of the areas in which people complement each other, and for which a sexual chemistry exists, is in the area of selfishness versus caring and giving to others. That is, people who are very selfish are attracted to individuals who are very giving. And vice versa—people who are very giving are sexually attracted to individuals who are very selfish.

It should be noted that all people in our society have a personality falling somewhere on a continuum between being extremely selfish to extremely giving to others. (Illustration)

Extremely Selfish   Extremely Giving

Ideally, it would be good for people to fall somewhere in the middle of this continuum, so that individuals in a romantic relationship can have as their complement someone who gives about 50%. The ideal, however, is not usually the case—but it would be good to avoid the extremes. That is, it would be good *not* to be someone who gives 90% in a relationship, and consequently falls in love with someone who gives only 10%, and vice-versa. Although the sexual experience could be quite intense, life goes on outside the bedroom and living with someone who gives only 10% in a relationship can be very frustrating and often leads to unhappiness.

You often see this pattern of marrying very selfish men in young girls who are very sweet and form romantic attachments very early in life. In the young, the hormones are raging, and choices are hastily made with an emphasis on the parts of the puzzle pieces that are opposite, creating a sexual chemistry. And not much emphasis is placed on the parts of the puzzle pieces that are similar, which would enable a friendship. The relationship may initially be great in bed, but it may wind up not being so great in day to day life.

If this relationship breaks up, most often the young girl goes on to repeat this same pattern in her next romantic attachment. (As with the example of Joanne, above.) That is, unfortunately, nice guys don't turn her on, and "bad guys" do. She is again attracted to rather selfish men, and they are attracted to her. It's as if a magnet exists between the two types of individuals. If she comes to a psychotherapist for help because she is continually frustrated in her romantic attachments, what should the psychotherapist do?

Hopefully this young lady chooses treatment with a cognitive-behavioral oriented psychotherapist rather than a psychoanalyst. Although Freud was brilliant in describing certain concepts, the effectiveness of psychoanalysis in treating this type of problem is sorely deficient. Classical psychoanalysis relies on insight, or having the client notice her repeated pattern of behavior, hoping that that will be sufficient to cause change. For example, in the treatment of Joanne, psychoanalysts may simply point out her repeated pattern of picking selfish men and hope that this awareness or insight would be sufficient to cause Joanne to choose nicer men in the future. Unfortunately, insight by itself is not sufficient. She's attracted to what she's attracted to. The old adage applies here: *"You can bring a horse to water, but you can't make it drink."* What is helpful about the jigsaw puzzle model of a romantic relationship is that it provides a template of what needs to be done: *TO CHANGE WHAT JOANNE IS ATTRACTED TO,* **SHE** *HAS TO CHANGE.*

FOR A WOMAN TO BE ATTRACTED TO MORE GIVING AND LESS SELFISH MEN, SHE HAS TO LEARN TO BECOME MORE SELFISH HERSELF. THAT IS, SHE HAS TO LEARN TO GIVE MORE TO HERSELF—THEN HER COMPLEMENT WILL BE A MORE CARING AND GIVING PERSON.

In effect, "the too giving person" has to move along the "selfish-giving" continuum illustrated above, to a more selfish position.

And how does a woman achieve this? A woman achieves this by learning to become more assertive and practicing it in her daily life.

Being assertive is stating what you feel and want—in an effort to get more of what you want in life. There are many books and manuals written covering the subject of assertiveness—with exercises individuals can practice to overcome deficiencies in assertiveness. A cognitive-behavioral oriented psychotherapist can also help an individual to become more assertive.

Many young women in our culture may have learned to not be very assertive, and to be too giving by the role model of a mother who was also too giving. And both may have learned it from a strict religious upbringing that taught them to "turn the other cheek" and put the other individual first. Regardless of where it was learned, a woman has to learn to become more *comfortably* selfish or more assertive if she is to be attracted to nicer men.

If the young lady who gives 90% in a romantic relationship and is attracted to men who give only 10% becomes more comfortably assertive to the extent that she gives less, for example 60% rather than 90%, she will be attracted to men who give 40% rather than 10%—and those nicer men will be attracted to her. Of course, the ideal would be 50/50, but we don't even have to have that degree of improvement for a woman to be attracted to nicer men. A romantic relationship where she is getting 40% is certainly better than getting 10% as in her previous relationship.

In women who start off in life being too nice, and learn from whatever experiences they have had that they need to take better care of themselves and be more assertive, we often see a progression in their romantic attachments in life to nicer, more giving men. Whether this change comes from learning from bad romantic experiences (the so-called "school of hard knocks"), or being in psychotherapy and learning to become more assertive; or whether this change is due to a diminution of sex drive as women age so that their romantic choices are dictated less by sexual attraction and more by friendship—this change is beneficial. Not being too nice, and being more comfortably assertive, helps people in general live a more satisfying life. This occurs not only in the romantic arena, but in other areas of one's life.

Although I have focused on women in this chapter, because in our culture this problem is more commonly seen in women, the problem of being too nice and romantically attracted to people who are not so nice, is seen in men as well as in women, and in gay as well as in straight relationships. The treatment of this problem through assertiveness applies to anyone who is romantically attracted to people who are too selfish, regardless of gender or sexual orientation.

However, if a person finds themselves in a romantic relationship or marriage with a rather selfish individual, it does not necessarily mean the relationship is doomed. To achieve a more satisfying relationship, the "too giving" individual needs to assert themselves in the relationship, and hope that their partner's emotional attachment to them will be sufficient to motivate their partner to move along the "selfish-giving" continuum to a more giving position. But, as a warning—old patterns of behavior are hard to change. Unfortunately, and to be frank, the "too giving" individual will have to keep up their assertiveness throughout their entire life with their romantic partner, otherwise their partner will very easily fall back into their previous too selfish behavior.

This chapter illustrates how the jigsaw puzzle model of a romantic relationship gives greater understanding of how choices are made in romantic attachments, and also provides a guide as to how to make the necessary changes that can lead to a more satisfying romantic relationship. Greater understanding of the dynamics of relationships, and consequently, constructive changes that can lead to more satisfying relationships, are the goals of this book.

BOTTOM LINE: In romantic relationships, one of the character traits in which people form a complementary sexual attraction is in the area of giving to others, versus selfishness. To be attracted to a more giving person one has to learn to become more comfortable giving to oneself, and less to others at one's expense.

ANGER
IN A ROMANTIC RELATIONSHIP

Samantha and Bill had been dating for a long time, but now they were bickering a lot. Did it mean they no longer loved each other? They were my patients in couples counseling, and I was a young psychiatric resident in training. I asked my supervisor for help. But his answer surprised me.

My supervisor answered my question by first asking *me* a question. What is the opposite of love, he asked me. I answered, "hate or anger." "**No**," he said, "the opposite of love is *indifference*." I was puzzled. He went on to explain that when two people love each other, they are emotionally interdependent. And when two people are emotionally dependent on one another, whatever one says or does has a much greater impact on their partner than the same thing said or done by a stranger. In fact, he said, you know when two people no longer love each other when what each says or does has **no** impact on the other. That is, when what each says or does is met with indifference. Thus, *the opposite of love is not anger or hate—but indifference*.

What my supervisor was telling me is that love and anger (or hate) are the flip sides of the same coin. You can't have one without the other. And it can, and will, surface from time to time.

In fact, over the years I've grown to learn that anger, when expressed in a romantic relationship, can be very constructive. Anger is an emotion indicating to the romantic partner that you're not happy with the current situation, and that you would like a change. It can be viewed as part of a statement of who you are and what's important to you. In effect, it's a greater exposure of your jigsaw puzzle piece than existed before the disagreement. The expression of anger in a romantic relationship implies that you're sufficiently attached to the other individual that you would like a change or an accommodation in the relationship, rather than a dissolution of the relationship.

As mentioned previously, in a romantic relationship it's better to define who you are, or the shape of your jigsaw puzzle piece sooner rather than later. If a romantic partner is right for you and sufficiently emotionally attached to you—and the accommodation asked for is not too large for that individual to make—your partner will accommodate and the relationship will survive. If the accommodation asked for *is* too large for that individual, the relationship will not survive and the relationship will break up. And if the relationship will not survive, it's better to know this sooner rather than later, and not waste anyone's time.

So, when something is upsetting you in a romantic relationship, you should express it. But you should try to express it in a constructive way, without putting your romantic partner down. Trying to insert the "I" word in your communication can be helpful to minimize the chances of making personal attacks and being judgmental. For example, by saying "I didn't like when you said that, or did that."

Unfortunately, one can expect in an intense emotional relationship, such as exists in a romantic relationship, occasional personal attacks or ad hominem statements. This should be pointed out in an effort to change the manner of communicating. But ultimately even *temporary* personal attacks should not be the cause of a breakup in a romantic relationship. We have to give a lot of slack within a romantic relationship. After all, it's an intense emotional experience, and people can get carried away. But violence, of course, is not acceptable. And partners who are habitually judgmental can be problematic in a romantic relationship. (See the chapter on "A Romantic Relationship with a Hypercritical Partner.")

There are many people who are uncomfortable with either receiving or expressing anger. This is a handicap in any intense relationship – whether it be a romantic relationship, a friendship, or an employer-employee relationship. As noted above, anger is an inseparable part of any interdependent relationship. And as a romantic relationship is the most intense of the interdependent personal relationships, having difficulty with anger – either expressing it or receiving it—will be a problem in developing and maintaining a romantic relationship.

Over the many years of practicing psychiatry, I have learned that there are a number of possible causes for an individual to have developed a discomfort with anger. They are:

- An individual who grew up in an environment where anger was followed by physical violence may fear that anger expressed could result in physical injury.

- If anger in the parental home was expressed irrationally—perhaps when a parent was drunk—an individual could feel if they were to express anger they would be viewed as "crazy" or "irrational."

- If anger preceded a divorce in the parental home, a person could fear expressing anger will automatically result in the ending of their romantic relationship.

- If an individual grew up in a home where anger was always delivered with the implication of a moral transgression, rather than something the parent didn't like, or didn't want their child to do, the individual may associate anger with the message that the recipient is "not a good person." And since the delivery of an angry statement is often followed by an angry retort, "not being a good person" is a message the individual in later life may not want to give *or* receive.

A PERSONAL ANECDOTE TO THE LAST POINT: I was very fortunate growing up. Not that anger was never expressed at home—on the contrary—it was expressed often. I was a very active child, and my mother would often get angry with me for my behavior. However, it was never delivered as a moral transgression. She understood that a child is basically a self-serving animal. As indeed, so is the parent. In my mother's eyes my behavior was normal human behavior. Our living together, however, necessitated some type of accommodation to our mutual needs and desires. A different parent could have handled it differently and have chastised me, calling me "selfish" when I put my desires first and did not consider or second guess her needs—and imply that I was not a good person. But since my mother deep down considered my behavior to be consistent with that of any normal human being, that type of communication was never delivered.

Regardless of the reason an individual may have difficulty expressing or receiving anger, it's a handicap – especially in a romantic relationship. And an effort should be made to overcome it.

If you have difficulty expressing anger in a romantic relationship, it may be helpful to remind yourself when you're angry that you're showing your partner how important your partner and your relationship are to you. When angry, repeating this mantra to yourself can be helpful: "*I'm **angry** and I care about you and our relationship enough to express it.*"

BOTTOM LINE: In any interdependent relationship anger will be felt from time to time. Since a romantic relationship is a very intense interdependent emotional relationship, it can especially be felt in a romantic relationship.

Expressing your anger is part of communicating who you are, and what's important to you. It defines the shape of your jigsaw puzzle piece for your partner to see. It can be very constructive. The relationship will either survive or it won't. And it's better to know sooner rather than later.

PUTTING PEOPLE DOWN
WHO ARE DIFFERENT THAN YOU ARE IS
NOT IN YOUR BEST INTEREST

We all know people who are habitually critical of other people. If you are in their company, they will gossip and find fault with practically everyone.

As the chapter on "Friendships" points out, as you go through life you will meet a lot of new people. Some people you will like more, and some people you will like less. The people you are more similar to, you will like more, and the people you are less similar to, you will like less. This is a normal reaction.

However, there are some people who have the tendency in general to "put down" or demean people who are different than themselves. They will come up with reasons for disliking an individual that are ultimately purely subjective. For example, they may verbalize their disapproval of the way an individual dresses or the manners or etiquette an individual demonstrates. These critical individuals pay very little attention to the fact that people are different—they are born with different talents, and are raised in different cultures. The bottom line is they are not very accepting of people who are different than themselves.

A PERSONAL ANECDOTE:

While standing on a long checkout line at a hotel I was staying at for a psychiatric convention in Manhattan, I heard one of my colleagues behind me say out loud, "She's so RUDE." And I wondered what he was talking about. Apparently, he was referring to the fact that the cashier was not engaging in pleasantries when a transaction was completed. She just yelled out "NEXT" to move the line along more quickly. (I frankly was pleased she was moving the line along so quickly.) However, this colleague lived far out in the horse country suburbs of Philadelphia, and that's not the way people spoke to each other there. He felt that she was rude. Well, being from New York City, I thought this was perfectly normal behavior, and I was shocked at his comment. Obviously, there was a difference in culture. I saw nothing wrong with the behavior that he thought was rude. My colleague, especially being a psychiatrist, I felt should have realized that people are different in the horse country suburbs of Philadelphia than they are in Manhattan. She was not rude… she was just a New Yorker.

Putting people down merely because they are different is not a good thing for a person to do for a number of reasons. First, there is a moral issue, and then there are more practical reasons.

Morally speaking, putting people down in the eyes of others merely because they behave in ways that are different than what you're used to, just doesn't seem like a nice thing to do. People are different and we should accept people as being different. These differences may be due to culture or genetics, but it doesn't mean these individuals are worth less than you, or have done anything wrong.

But there are more self-serving reasons to be more accepting of others. In mixed company, *if you voice criticism of others not present, people around you will assume, consciously or unconsciously, that you could just as well be critical of THEM when THEY'RE not around. People may not express it, but people are uncomfortable around individuals who are habitually critical and non-accepting of others.* And if your goal is to meet new people for either a friendship or a possible romantic relationship, people avoiding you because they are fearful you could be critical of them is not helpful.

There is also an important psychological concept that has relevance here. This is the concept of "projection." Projection is the normal tendency to assume that others see things the way you do. This is a perfectly normal human reaction. And it can work for you, or against you. *If you're the kind of person who is generally accepting of others, you will assume others you meet will generally be accepting of you. And, as a result, you'll be more comfortable meeting new people. But if you're the kind of person who habitually finds fault with others and is critical of the people you meet—whether you just think it or express it—you will automatically assume that the people you meet will readily find fault with you.* The latter manner of thinking unfortunately causes critical people to be shy and avoid meeting new people. And if your goal is to meet new people in the hopes of establishing a new relationship, being shy and avoiding new people is not helpful in achieving that goal.

Another problem for critical individuals is their sensitivity to criticism itself. Critical people are themselves individuals who are the *most* sensitive to receiving criticism. When individuals who are generally very accepting of others receive criticism, they are more likely to register it as someone else's opinion, rather than as a fact. A critical person, however, tends to see the world in absolute terms – right or wrong, good or bad—and views the criticism he or she receives in an absolute manner, rather than just someone else's opinion, and is consequently more easily offended.

This extreme sensitivity to criticism in critical individuals has its consequences in forming and maintaining friendships. Like anyone else, a critical person will be attracted as a friend to people who are similar to themselves—that is, people who are habitually critical of others. And since critical people will do what critical people do—that is be critical of others—including possibly their friends—their friendships often don't last very long, especially since their friends are also people who are very sensitive to receiving criticism. (How often have you heard a critical person say, "I'm not going to speak to HER anymore!"?)

Thus, habitually critical people face a lot of obstacles forming close relationships. Not only do they tend to be avoided by people in general, but they avoid new people themselves because they unconsciously anticipate and fear criticism. (They anticipate criticism due to projection.) In addition, since they are more easily offended by criticism than the average person, their relationships tend to be short-lived and unstable. A critical individual can wind up being quite lonely.

In a romantic relationship, a critical person will tend to be sexually attracted to someone who is more accepting of others. But this relationship is often fraught with discomfort as the non-critical partner finds it very uncomfortable living with someone who constantly finds fault with them. It's a relationship fraught with angst. And indeed, it may break up. This topic will be discussed in greater depth in the next chapter.

Thus, if you are a critical person, it's worth trying to change. Especially since the person you may be the *most* critical of is someone you spend a great deal of time with—*yourself.*

Unfortunately, changing a person's habitual way of thinking is easier said than done. It's not easy for a critical person (or any person) to change a lifelong pattern of thinking. Most likely these individuals had at least one parent who modeled being super critical.

One of the ways critical people can work at trying to change is to practice "self-talk." When these individuals find themselves internally putting down someone who is different, they could follow that thought with a more accepting one. For example, if you find yourself thinking negatively about someone who doesn't coordinate clothes well, you could say to yourself "Well, not everyone is born with the talent to see how clothes coordinate. It's a talent." Or, "Perhaps that's the way they dress where this individual is from." It's also helpful to remind yourself that the individual you're criticizing may have talents and strengths in areas where you have relative weakness.

Ultimately, we have to remember that we're all a product of our genes and our environment. And ultimately. we're all in the same boat – doing the best we can to achieve what we want. And what people want in life is not that different among different people. We need to be more accepting of others who are different.

BOTTOM LINE: Habitually being critical and judgmental of others works against you in establishing stable, long-lasting relationships. If you have this characteristic, you should try to change it.

A ROMANTIC RELATIONSHIP WITH A HYPERCRITICAL PARTNER

Often people find themselves in a romantic relationship with someone who is very critical. This critical individual may find fault in their partner with practically everything their partner does. Indeed, and amazingly, this individual can find fault with the very personality characteristics that attracted him or her to their partner in the first place. An example is a patient I treated many years ago:

> Susan was an attractive young lady in her twenties. She came to me feeling very depressed. She had just been rejected by a young man she had dated for over a year. She said she wanted to work on changing the things that caused her boyfriend to reject her. Among his many complaints were that Susan was "very emotional," "always late," and "very forgetful." When upset with her, he would describe her as "a complete mess."

> Steve, Susan's boyfriend, was a successful and handsome young attorney. He was a very focused individual who took pride in his work, and in never being late and always being prepared and organized. Although critical of Susan, he confided to her that every girl he dated prior to Susan had the same problems she had. Consequently, their relationship never lasted very long. He was very frustrated.

Getting to know Susan, it was apparent that Susan had Attention Deficit Disorder, a syndrome we see in many individuals. Individuals with Attention Deficit Disorder, or ADD for short, have trouble focusing and are very distractible. They can be quite forgetful, and being organized is challenging for them. However, on the flip side, individuals with ADD have very many positive character traits. They tend to be very much in touch with their feelings, very sensitive to the world around them, outgoing, friendly, and very creative. Individuals with ADD characteristically see things which others miss in a situation, and bring to the table new ways of looking at things. Individuals with ADD often work in the arts. Those individuals in the sciences who have a "touch" of ADD are often the most successful in their field, because they can bring creativity into their scientific work.

Using our jigsaw puzzle model of romantic relationships—where opposite characteristics create a sexual chemistry—it could be predicted that Steve, a very focused and organized individual, would be sexually attracted to women similar to Susan—that is, young ladies with ADD. However, where Steve differs from other young men with his obsessive character traits is that Steve, a very critical person by nature, tends to be critical of the very characteristics that attracted him to these young women in the first place.

What causes Steve to be overly-critical? As with other overly-critical individuals, most likely he was brought up by an overly-critical parent. But regardless of the cause, when this tendency of being very critical exists, it's very hard to change, and creates problems in romantic relationships—as well as in other relationships. Individuals who are overly critical tend to have problems with their friendships as well as in the workplace.

For example, in the workplace, Steve's subordinates could find themselves feeling disheartened if their work was found never good enough. And most likely they would want to leave, and find work elsewhere. If Steve were to have children and be very critical of them, they could experience feelings of helplessness, worthlessness, and depression.

Unlike an employee who can quit, children are stuck in their home and in their relationships—that is, until they are older. These young adults would be the first to want to go to an out-of-town college, or move into their own apartment.

Ultimately, if a person is in a dependent relationship with a hypercritical person—whether that dependent relationship is an emotional one (as with a romantic partner or child), or a financial one (as with a spouse, child or employee)—over a period of time that criticism is *INTERNALIZED by the dependent individual*. That is, individuals get to *FEEL* that which is said about them is TRUE. And low self-esteem and depression will follow.

This is what happened to Susan in her relationship with Steve. She felt depressed and her self-esteem was devastated by Steve's constant criticism. And she was criticized for things that were very hard for her to change, because it was part of her nature.

In a romantic relationship, it may take time for a hypercritical individual to demonstrate their true personality. Most likely, subconsciously these individuals recognize their problem and restrain their criticism in the courting phase of their relationship. That is, they restrain themselves until they feel more comfortable and in control, and then their true personality comes out.

In Susan's therapy, it took a while, but Susan improved. She understood that Steve's personality was that of habitually being a very critical person. Understanding the jigsaw puzzle model of a romantic relationship and Steve's personality, it was possible to see that he could be one of those individuals who would be critical of *any* girl with whom he formed a romantic attachment. Susan came to realize that although she had ADD and had to deal with the challenges that condition presented, along with ADD came a lot of very positive character traits. Though Susan would have the tendency to again be attracted romantically to obsessive men—and they to her—not every man who has obsessive character traits would be a very critical person. With time, Susan's self-esteem rose, and she started dating again. And then she met Bob.

Bob was a financial analyst who worked on Wall Street. One day, Susan came into her therapy session very excited. She recounted a story about her new boyfriend.

Susan threw a dinner party to introduce Bob to her friends. However, as was often the case with Susan, she was running late from the creative job she loved. After having rushed to the supermarket to buy groceries, she was now in the kitchen frantically trying to put together all the ingredients to make dinner *when suddenly the doorbell rang.* It was Bob, who had come early. Susan became very anxious. "Oh my God," she said to herself. "He'll see this mess and think I'm such a ditz." Unfortunately, the self-critical thoughts she had learned from her ex-boyfriend, Steve, came rushing back to her. But Bob came in, saw the mess, and gave an affectionate laugh. "Okay," he said, "we'll make like a magician and get this all together." He pitched in and it turned out to be a wonderful dinner party.

At her session, Susan remarked that if that had been Steve, he would have been very angry and all over her with criticism. He would have said, *"How could you? You knew you had guests coming. "Why didn't you pay more attention to time? You're really so irresponsible and inconsiderate."* He would have given no heed to the fact that Susan was the kind of young lady who would be so enthusiastically involved with the job she loved, that she would easily lose track of time and run late. But Bob was *attracted* to these characteristics. Why would he put her down for them? As with Steve, Bob was a very focused individual. (And perhaps on some level he may have felt that he was *too* focused.) Bob appreciated a young lady who could live in the moment and was full of life. Why would he criticize the very character traits that attracted him in the first place? It was at this session that Susan realized that this was the kind of guy she would like to marry. And she did.

The last time I saw Susan, she was happily wheeling a baby carriage.

By the way, while Susan was dating Bob, Steve called and tried to rekindle their relationship. But Susan was not interested. She found someone she loved, and who loved her, and accepted her just the way she was.

It should be pointed out, that unless Steve changes, he's going to continue to have problems with his romantic relationships. Although Steve responds normally to his romantic interests, his tendency to put women down for the very characteristics that turned him on to begin with will ultimately lead to the unhappiness of his girlfriends as well as himself. Most likely Steve will eventually marry. But his future wife will have a hard time. His tendency to repeatedly criticize her will affect her self-esteem, their relationship, and ultimately his *OWN* happiness. Unfortunately, his wife will turn out to be the kind of woman I often saw in my office discussing an unhappy marriage.

It takes time for an individual to realize they are in a romantic relationship with a hypercritical person. As mentioned, in the courting phase of a romantic relationship a critical person often does not show his or her true colors. Only when this individual feels comfortable and sufficiently in control of the relationship does this individual let go and reveal his or her true personality. By that time, however, for many people it may be too late. For example, it may be a young woman who was seduced by the romance, perhaps eager to marry, already has children and does not feel the liberty to separate.

Being a very critical person by nature is not easy to change. As mentioned previously, usually these individuals were raised by a hypercritical parent, who were themselves raised by a hypercritical parent, and so on, and so forth—going back for many generations. If you happen to find yourself in a romantic relationship with a hypercritical person, it's best to move on—if you can.

If you feel stuck in a romantic relationship with a hypercritical person, such as in a marriage where you feel for objective reasons you can't leave, it's best to keep this individual on what I describe as "a short leash." You have to remember that this individual who is critical of you is also emotionally attached to you and consequently dependent on you. You have to use the power you have and be assertive, just as hopefully you were in the courting phase of your relationship, when you felt more independent and in control, and when your partner was less secure and probably less critical. Unfortunately, it's a lot of work—which runs contrary to the ideal in a romantic relationship. The ideal romantic relationship should require very little work. The less the work, the better the relationship.

BOTTOM LINE: Some people are hypercritical as part of their personality. Amazingly, these individuals can criticize the very character traits that attracted them to their romantic partner in the first place. This can result in an unhappy romantic relationship—and if a person marries such an individual—an unhappy living situation and marriage. It's best to avoid this type of individual if you can.

THE BREAKUP OF A COMMITTED ROMANTIC RELATIONSHIP

The jigsaw puzzle model of a romantic relationship predicts long-term stability when two criteria are met: the two individuals *complement* each other in certain characteristics—to create a sexual attraction—and when there are sufficient *similarities* in the two individuals—to create a friendship. So how do we explain a breakup in a long-term committed relationship?

The following are possible explanations for the breakup of a long term committed romantic relationship:

1. NOT KNOWING EACH OTHER WELL ENOUGH: There are some people who are very slow to reveal themselves. This may be due to shyness, low self-esteem, or deliberately not showing one's "true colors" for fear of being rejected and the relationship not working. Ultimately, however, one's true nature is revealed, especially when people live with each other for a while. Then the discovery can be made that the shape of a partner's jigsaw puzzle piece that was fantasized was not real. And the fit and match is not there.

   An example of the above may very well have been the case with the late Princess Diana and Prince Charles of England. A rather shy young lady, courted by a man who would later become King of England, one could readily imagine how Diana may have had difficulty showing who she was. It is my assumption that only upon being married and living together did Charles and Diana realize that they were not right for each other. Ultimately, Charles preferred a woman whom many people felt was not as attractive as Diana, but obviously was the right fit and match for him.

It is interesting to note that the Queen of England, probably the most conservative woman in the world, did not object or put an end to her grandson Prince William, also a future King of England, living with his then-girlfriend, Kate Middleton. One could suspect, by way of the divorce of two of her sons shortly after marrying, that the Queen realized the importance of people knowing each other well before marrying. As expressed in her speech to Parliament, she probably did not want another *"annus horribilis."*

2. TOO MUCH EMPHASIS ON THE SEXUAL COMPONENT IN A ROMANTIC RELATIONSHIP, AND NOT ENOUGH EMPHASIS ON THE FRIENDSHIP COMPONENT: The tendency to emphasize sex versus friendship in a romantic relationship is especially seen in young individuals, as the hormone levels in the young are quite high.

An example of emphasizing sex over friendship was given in the chapter "Being Too Nice is Not Good." As discussed in that chapter, people who are overly nice are sexually attracted to people who are overly selfish, and vice versa. (The characteristic of being overly nice is more commonly seen in women in our culture.) Although the sexual chemistry, or the "fit," may initially be very strong, the "match," or the friendship component, may be sorely deficient. That is, living with an overly selfish individual is not very pleasant, as this individual winds up not being a very good friend—especially a friend you want to live with. If the more giving partner asks for more accommodation in the relationship, and the more selfish partner doesn't accommodate, the relationship could very well break up. If the overly accommodative partner—usually the female partner—doesn't have the ability to assert herself, and abruptly ends the relationship, she may go on to repeat this pattern in the next gentleman she is attracted to. (Men who are not nice are attractive to her – until she lives with them or marries them, and finds out that they're not very good friends—and eventually separates.)

3. PEOPLE CHANGE: People may not change very much, but when they do, the shape of their jigsaw puzzle piece changes, and consequently so does the right fit and match for these individuals in a romantic relationship.

There are times when a person in a long-lasting romantic relationship or a marriage becomes too accommodative with the passage of time, and thus becomes less of the individual they were when they first became romantically involved. Perhaps due to their greater financial dependence, especially if children are involved, this is more commonly seen in women in our society. When this occurs, the gentleman partner may lose interest in his wife, drift apart emotionally and may even separate. (In the interim, he may even have had an affair.) In most cases, if the wife becomes more assertive and regains her identity, the husband will snap back, becoming more aware of his attachment to his wife, and the original fit and match will return. The bottom line is that a person shouldn't lose themselves in a relation-ship. Assertiveness is very important in establishing and maintaining one's self.

Assertiveness is important in defining the shape of one's jig-saw puzzle piece. It expresses what you want, and what's important to you. It expresses your needs, wants, values, in-terests, etc. Ultimately, it presents who you are. Romantic relationships can drift or fall apart when an individual has difficulty being assertive, and maintaining his or her identity.

When an individual becomes less assertive in a romantic relationship, for any reason, their romantic partner may take advantage of the situation (consciously or uncon-sciously), fill this gap, and become a less considerate indi-vidual. The less assertive individual (usually the female partner) may be tempted to leave the romantic relationship and find someone else. To this individual I usually say, "*Walk away, don't run away.*" That is, try asserting yourself first to see if your partner will become sufficiently accom-modative to your satisfaction such that breaking up is not necessary. If your assertiveness has not achieved sufficient accommodation to generate your satisfaction, leaving the relationship would then be *walking away*, rather than run-ning away. If you have not tried asserting yourself first be-fore breaking up a romantic relationship, you would be *run-ning away* rather than walking away.

There are times, however, people may form a romantic re-lationship when a temporary situation exists. When the temporary situation no longer exists, the fit and match of their romantic partner may no longer be the best choice for them. In effect, the individual has changed, and so has the shape of their jigsaw puzzle piece. An example of this could have been the case with the ex-presidential candidate and senator Robert Dole and his first wife.

Senator Robert Dole had a tragic military injury which left his right arm and hand disfigured, and limited in functioning. His first wife was an occupational therapist in a hospital where he was treated. In his autobiography, Bob Dole wrote of his first wife: "(She) made me forget my injuries. She helped me think not in terms of disability, but of ability. She treated me like everyone else." Occupational therapists are generally very positive and supportive in their thinking and behavior, and no doubt his first wife provided Bob Dole with what he was lacking at that time. However, when he learned to accept and accommodate to his disability, and his old personality returned, his first wife's personality may not have been the best fit and match for him. His second wife, Elizabeth Dole, the ex-head of the American Red Cross, may have been a more suitable relationship when his self-confidence returned.

Sometimes alcohol or drugs become a problem in a relationship that didn't exist during the courtship phase of a romantic relationship. When you speak to the spouse of an alcoholic, the response is often "They're not the same person when they're drinking." If they're not the same person, then the shape of their jigsaw puzzle piece has changed, and thus, so has the best fit and match for them. Unless the substance-abusing person enters recovery, the relationship could very well fall apart. Indeed, the whole concept of Al-Anon is based on the spouse of the drug abuser becoming more of an independent, assertive individual, which may have the effect of bouncing their partner into abstinence and the shape of the puzzle piece the drug abusing partner had before they married. If not, the Al-Anon participant may very well "walk away."

4. PEOPLE MAY HAVE "SETTLED" IN THEIR CHOICE OF A ROMANTIC PARTNER: Our jigsaw puzzle model of a romantic relationship states that if it "fits" for one side, it "fits" for the other side. And the degree of "fit" will be equal for both parties in the relationship. There are times, however, that people may have chosen to settle for a romantic relationship that was *mutually* not a very high degree of fit and match. For example, there may have been limited choices available in the small town where the two individuals grew up, and their romantic relationship was the best the two could come up with. Years pass, and individuals in this situation could lead a happy life with children and a network of friends. However, if by chance there is exposure by one of the romantic partners to a person not known before, that is a better fit and match for that individual, this partner could be tempted to break up their committed relationship. Most often, however, because sexual drive is lower with age, and family and friends are entrenched, an individual will choose not to act on this discovery and break up their primary relationship. But occasionally a breakup may happen, in which case it's unfortunate for the romantic partner that has been left behind. Because of life's circumstances (age, children, limited exposure to potential romantic partners), he or she may not have many options available for a suitable replacement.

5. A ROMANTIC RELATIONSHIP COMPOSED OF A GAY AND A STRAIGHT INDIVIDUAL: A romantic relationship consisting of a gay and a straight individual

could last for many years, but could ultimately break up if one of individuals is gay and decides to leave the relationship. (This topic was discussed briefly in the chapter "Being Rejected in a Romantic Relationship.")

The straight individual may feel their partner is the right fit and match for them, and question the validity of our rule about romantic relationships. But ***our rule that if an individual knows their romantic partner well, and feels that their partner is the right fit and match for them, their partner will feel the same way, DOES NOT APPLY if one of the individuals in the relationship is gay. For the gay individual, their romantic partner is the WRONG GENDER.*** (For the straight individual, their romantic partner *IS* the right gender.)

Some gay men and women claim they were not aware of their sexual orientation until after they were married. If the gay partner chooses to break up their relationship after this discovery, and after having spent many years together, it leaves the straight partner at a great disadvantage—especially if there are children. For the straight individual, there are fewer alternative partners available compared to when they were younger and single. If this early lack of awareness of one's sexual orientation by the gay partner is caused by an unconscious denial of one's sexual orientation due to the prejudices of society, hopefully this lack of self-awareness will diminish as society becomes more tolerant. Certainly, it is a strong argument for more tolerance considering the hardships that often result from this type of breakup.

Jack Almeleh, M.D.

BOTTOM LINE: Not all committed romantic relationships are stable. And they could fall apart for a number of reasons. A number of these reasons are discussed in this chapter.